Call Back Yesterday

"O, call back yesterday, bid time return"
Richard II

My grateful thanks to those who helped me call back yesterday, especially Than, Will, Cynthia and Edith.

CALL BACK YESTERDAY

Sarah E. Francis

The Pentland Press
Edinburgh – Cambridge – Durham

First published in 1994
by The Pentland Press Ltd
1 Hutton Close
South Church
Bishop Auckland
Durham

ISBN 1-85821-214-6

Typeset by Carnegie Publishing Ltd, 18 Maynard St, Preston
Printed and bound by Antony Rowe Ltd, Chippenham

For Nick,
with my love

Contents

CHAPTER 1

Moscow, 1989

"Wake oop! Wake oop! Time. Anglesi – Time – Wake oop!"

Than surfaced from a heavy sleep to find himself being shaken violently. For a moment or two he wondered where he was. The lumpy mattress on which he was lying convinced him that he was neither at home nor in his luxurious New York suite. He opened his eyes.

A small, elderly babushka had him in her grip. Her wrinkled face looked cross.

"You wake, Anglesi. Wake."

When Than had asked for an early morning call at his Moscow hotel he had not envisaged being roused in such a manner.

"Thank you! Merci! Danke!" He had never managed to get his tongue round the Russian language.

1

After the old lady had gone Than got out of bed. In spite of the fact that he was going home that day he felt incredibly depressed. He noticed that each time he came to, and left, this beautiful, benighted city of Moscow he had the same reactions.

He arrived with the adrenalin flowing and ready to tackle any problems presented by the job which awaited him. Over the weeks the effort of communicating technical data through an interpreter, the red tape and incompetence of officials, the meetings arranged with ministers when nobody turned up, all wore down his optimism and dampened his natural cheerfulness. Each time he left for home feeling that he had made very little progress in spite of his efforts.

Than went into the bathroom and looked at the lavatory on its rocky stand. He surveyed the half-dozen towels, thin as tea towels and not much bigger, which were supposed to serve his drying needs. He seemed to hear the voice of his sister, Lantie, saying, "Now, Than, when you go to Russia, be sure to take a couple of big bath towels, some soap and plenty of lavatory paper with you. And be careful if you have to visit the public loos when you are out and about. In some places, even in the cities, you need to be wearing Wellington boots to enter them."

Than smiled and reflected that Lantie thought herself an expert on matters Russian after a couple of visits to that country. She had always been a bossy boots but was often right. He carried soap with him but invariably forgot the towels and lavatory paper. The latter in most Moscow hotels was so coarse that he thought torn pages of *Pravda* might have been softer.

Years of comfortable living in the United States had not prepared Than for roughing it in Moscow. Even at one hundred pounds a night, his present abode was far from luxurious. He had a double room which meant that two bunk beds were nailed together by the feet, making a long structure against one wall.

On each bed was a knitted duvet with an oval hole in the middle. As the weather grew colder or warmer the hole was used to stuff pieces of cloth and rags into the covering, making the duvet thicker or thinner as required.

After he had washed and dressed, Than packed his bags and looked at his watch. He knew that it was no use going downstairs for breakfast until eight o'clock. The old dragon who sat at a desk outside the door of the dining room and inspected residents' passes, would not let him in a minute before time.

He checked that he had a carton of two hundred American cigarettes at the top of his hold-all. Than recalled his first visit to Moscow. He had flown from Berlin and was seated on the plane next to a friendly German. When the Duty Free trolley came along the aisle the German bought two hundred cigarettes.

"For you, too?" he enquired politely.

"I don't smoke," replied Than.

"Were I you, friend, I would buy some cigarettes of the American kind. Unless, that is, you wish to walk from the airport into Moscow. The cab drivers will not take roubles, only hard currency and they all want American cigarettes as well. If we can arrange with two other passengers perhaps we can pay in dollars or marks and give only one carton of cigarettes."

Than remembered his first journey from the airport into Moscow: four hefty Westerners crammed themselves and their luggage into a Lada. The jokes about breathing in turn gave way to sharp intakes of breath and occasional swear words at the cabbie's standard of driving.

As Than stood by the window and gazed out he could see the domes and rooftops of the Kremlin. He thought himself fortunate to have a room where the windows had been cleaned. The hotel was twenty storeys high and the windows of the top seventeen floors had never been cleaned except by the rain and snow. There were no cradles or modern window cleaning equipment available to reach beyond the third floor. The dirt, aggravated by the ravages of the weather, gave the upper windows the appearance of frosted glass. He opened the door of his room, looked outside and closed it again. On each landing there were upholstered settees and through the glass swing doors a security guard was on duty at a desk. The desk was manned twenty-four hours a day. The officer on duty checked passes, made notes or spent his time reading.

Every night the Moscow hookers occupied the settees. They plied their trade whilst the duty officer sat impassively at the desk or chatted to them to relieve the boredom. Than wondered if these ladies, 'butterflies of the night' as they were known, had passes to gain entrance to the hotel. He assumed that they must find customers amongst the hard currency residents. Someone had told him that a doctor in Moscow earned an average salary of a hundred pounds a month, whilst some hookers could make a thousand pounds a month in their profession. They were extremely well dressed and some were very beautiful. By morning the landings were empty except for the ubiquitous security guard.

Yet there was much that Than liked and admired about Moscow. He was impressed by Red Square and its architecture as well as that of many other buildings in the city. He found the edifice that housed the Gumm Store and many of the museums and churches very impressive. He marvelled at the fantastic Metro stations where the trains seemed to run like clockwork as if drawn on an invisible thread.

After his initial visit to Moscow, when he had worked hard to break down the barriers of suspicion and prejudice which were raised by the officials, Than found himself accepted with a certain reserved friendliness. Sometimes a minister or high ranking bureaucrat would offer him the use of a chauffeur-driven car and tickets to the Bolshoi Ballet or the theatre. He and two or three western colleagues enjoyed these privileges.

Occasionally they sent the chauffeur home and walked back to their hotel through streets that were quiet by western standards. They tried to find their way about the Metro, guessing the direction, and counting the stations because they could not read the place names.

As eight o'clock approached Than set off for the dining room. He knew what breakfast would be even before the dragon had ticked him off her list and allowed him to go beyond her desk. The menu of salami, boiled eggs, black bread, yoghurt or sour milk seldom varied. He enjoyed the black bread but was sick of salami and boiled eggs.

The coffee samovar, which stood on a sideboard, was made of stainless steel. The tap was loose and tied up with a piece of rag. That rag, which irritated Than every morning, encapsulated for him what was wrong with Russia. Nothing worked properly, nobody fixed anything and nobody cared.

There was no unemployment but many of the employed did little or no work. He was tired of hearing the old joke, 'They pretend to pay us so we pretend to work'. He never ceased to be amazed at the massive waste of talents and resources.

Than found the corruption and the graft were even more frustrating than the inertia. On one of his visits home he explained his feelings to Lantie who was interested in all aspects of his environment.

"I know when I have a meal I am going to be ripped off. It galls me that when I pay the waiter, he calmly sorts out the money and puts part of it in his back pocket before he takes the rest to the till. The official rate of exchange is ten roubles to the pound but they charge us a hundred roubles because we can never find anyone to give us the real rate."

Than knew that the journey home would not be an easy one. He had been unable to get a direct flight from Moscow to London. Instead he was booked to fly to Stockholm where he would catch a plane to Heathrow.

After breakfast he collected his bags, settled his bill and went outside to barter with the taxi drivers who were loitering around the hotel door. On his way to Moscow's Sheremetyevo Airport he saw the street sellers and wondered how they made enough for a bare existence. The little old men and women who came in from the country to sell a few cucumbers seemed permanent fixtures. On the other hand it was evident that spring had come. Flower sellers had lilac, lilies of the valley and blooms from the far south of Russia on display.

There were even one or two men with small boxes selling ice creams. Than never forgot his surprise during an early visit to the city when he saw customers queuing for ice-creams. Some bought three bars and stood and ate them one after the other. On enquiring about this odd behaviour he learned that the buyers were limited to three ice creams each and as they did not know when they would see any more they scoffed the ration on the spot.

He looked out of the taxi window at the queue that stretched round two blocks from MacDonalds. A queue had formed from the first day of the opening of the restaurant and it seemed to get longer as the days passed. Young Russian entrepreneurs used to line up very early in the day. After being served they would take their purchases far back down the queue and sell them for double the price they had paid.

The airport was shabby, smelly and chaotic with frustrated passengers all seemingly going nowhere. Than was unsurprised when he reached the information desk to discover that his plane would be over an hour late. He checked in and went to the coffee bar. There he was further annoyed to find that it was closed. As it was the only one in the whole precinct he was obliged to go into the restaurant.

He sat down at a table and waited. He was very tired and was beginning to feel every one of his sixty years. There were plenty of waitresses about, but none of them bothered to come over and take his order. He opened his wallet and took out a ten dollar bill which he held in the air. Immediately a waitress hurried over. Smiling and speaking excellent English she wrote down his order. The choice was not wide, so he settled for sausages and pickled cucumber, black bread and coffee.

When he paid the bill he gave the waitress the ten dollar bill as a tip. She thanked him volubly and her smile widened at such munificence.

At last his flight was called and he boarded the Aeroflot. The plane seemed almost new which was a relief as the airline had not a good record and so far he had managed to avoid travelling on Russian planes.

At least it was not an internal flight. These were often cancelled because of fuel shortages. Sometimes the lucrative international

6

flights were held up until they had a good load on board. Than hoped there would be enough passengers on this flight for a quick take-off.

There were only three other people in the First Class section, a Swiss and two Americans. Than sat in a seat next to a window and they talked amongst themselves in a desultory way while waiting for the plane to take off. After what seemed an interminable time they left Sheremetyevo and became airborne. They fell to discussing the enormous difficulties of the task of modernising the Soviet Union.

"This guy, Gorbachev, he's sure got problems," said one of the Americans. "He's got the right ideas but he's up against a brick wall."

Each of them had his own fund of stories of muddle, corruption and incompetence; yet the general consensus was that things were changing very slowly and would continue to change over a period of years.

Than made the others laugh with some anecdotes about his time in America.

"You think there are some weird things happening in Russia. I've had my share of oddballs in the States," he said.

He told them how, at one time, he was Director of Engineering in charge of a huge reconstruction programme at a famous New York hotel.

"It was one of those places which took up a whole block with doors on the streets at the back and front. Every man and his dog used to take a short cut through the place and this posed quite a security problem. There were two thousand bedrooms and most of them were filled nearly all the time.

"From time to time I was Duty Manager and it was one darned thing after another. Usually I was on call with my chief engineer, a great guy with a marvellous sense of humour. One night we had word that a fellow was running round the hotel stark naked. Charlie and I and a couple of porters set off on the chase and finally we cornered him on the tenth floor. Instead of giving himself up he made for an open lift shaft and leapt inside. Fortunately for him it was a laundry chute. He dropped down several floors and landed on a pile of dirty linen. Then all we had to do was to get to the basement and haul out the linen until we reached him. By that time the cops had arrived and we draped him in bath towels so that he could be escorted away in some decency." The other men laughed, but Than had not finished his tale.

"On another occasion, no sooner had Charlie settled down in my suite for a quiet drink when we had a panic call. One of the cleaners had had a heart attack and seemed to be dead. We followed the usual drill: 'Call the cops, then call the medics'. The cops came and pronounced her dead and covered her with a sheet. On their heels came the medics who, after a quick examination, said she was alive and drew back the sheet. 'Dead,' declared the cops, pulling the sheet over her head again. 'Alive, shouted a doctor, pulling it down. If it hadn't been so serious it would have been hilarious; it was like slap-stick comedy. However, alive she was and the doctors took her off to hospital. Unfortunately she died the next morning, but the doctors had had their moment of triumph.

"Once again, when Charlie was on duty, we had an emergency call in the early hours of the morning. We dashed up to a room on the twelfth floor where we found a woman having hysterics and her husband lying dead on the bed. Unhappily, it turned out that he wasn't her husband, which partially accounted for the hysterics. 'He mustn't be found in my room, Get him out!' she kept saying between her sobs.

"We had a quick discussion and Charlie dashed down to the reception computer and soon came back with details of an empty single room on the same floor. Our hearts were in our mouths as we carried the corpse to the empty room and made him comfortable in bed. Then we transferred his belongings and put his clothes in the wardrobe and made everything appear natural. We had to leave him for the cleaners to find because we would not have been able to account for knowing about him. Dead men can't ring for room service.

"Charlie checked him into the room and altered the computer details of the original entry. The woman checked out early in the morning and as soon as we heard that the cops and medics had arrived we knew all would be well. Whew! I never want experiences like that again whether in New York or Moscow."

His fellow passengers laughed immoderately and one of the Americans said, "You couldn't have got away with moving a dead mouse in any of the Moscow hotels. Though I doubt if anyone saw a mouse they would rouse themselves to do anything about it."

Than began to feel very warm and took out his handkerchief to mop himself. He dropped it on the floor and reached down to pick it up. His hand touched the side of the aircraft and he leapt back and swore. The fuselage of the plane was red hot.

"Feel this," he said to the others.

"Say, it's cooking. Must be the electrics!" exclaimed one of the Americans. "This stretch is the same."

"Perhaps we ought to tell the stewardess," suggested Than.

"Have you seen her?" asked the Swiss.

At that moment a stewardess hove into sight. She was huge in size and her uniform made her look intimidating.

"You tell her," said the Swiss.

"No, you," urged Than.

She bore down upon them.

"What is it that you want?" she demanded. Than and the Swiss looked at each other.

"Two vodkas, please," said Than meekly.

The aircraft became uncomfortably hot and they all removed their jackets and ties. They decided there was nothing they could do about the overheated fuselage. It was in the lap of the gods whether they arrived in Stockholm or not. They dredged up old Aeroflot jokes they had heard from time to time.

"Isn't that the airline where they have outside toilets?"

"This is the captain speaking. We are losing height, please pedal harder."

The vodkas kept coming and the voices and laughter grew louder under the disapproving eye of the stewardess. Food, they were given to understand, would be served later, much later. They relaxed and began to exchange life stories.

"Would you believe me if I told you that I was named after a character in the Bible?" asked one American.

"Yeah! Tobias and all his angels were the inspiration for my name. I play it dumb and everyone calls me Toby."

"I had an Uncle Tobias years ago," recalled Than. "He was a real character, a true eccentric. I guess I never really appreciated him until after he was gone."

After a while the talking died down and the heat and the effects of the vodka took over. Than followed the example of the others, made himself as comfortable as possible and fell asleep.

CHAPTER 2

Summer, 1939

"Than! Don't you dare speak to your Uncle Tobias in that tone of voice."

"Sorry, Uncle Tobias," muttered Than. "But it's not fair! Why can't I have some long trousers? Everybody has them."

"I've told you why a dozen times," retorted Mama. "You are not old enough to go into long trousers. Twelve is quite soon enough for a boy to have them. In any case, you couldn't wear them at school. Your uniform list says that boys must wear short trousers until the age of twelve."

"Can't I have some for Sundays and best?" pleaded Than.

"Certainly not! you'd be the laughing stock of Priors Ings. Now I don't want to hear any more about it. Go and get washed and

changed and be off to Choir Practice. Long trousers indeed! Whatever next!"

As Than went out of the living room his sister Lantie appeared.

"Mama – – – – –" she began.

"No," interrupted Mama. "I've said 'No' and I mean it. I've never
heard of such an outrageous idea. Wanting to go pea picking! We
shall see what your Poppa has to say about it when he comes home.
He will soon put an end to that nonsense. You and Jeanie should be
able to find plenty to do during her visit without going pea picking."

"But, Mama – – – – –."

"I've said my last word on the matter," said Mama crossly. "Now
I don't want to hear any more about it. You two children will turn
my hair as white as wool before you have finished."

"It's not fair!" shouted Lantie. "I can't do anything in this house."
She flung herself out and stamped up the stairs to her bedroom where
she slammed the door so hard the noise reverberated through the
house.

"One day that lass will break every window in this place with her
slamming and banging," grumbled Uncle Tobias who was trying to
read the paper. "There's not a minute's peace with those two children. If it isn't one it's the other having tantrums an' such like."

Uncle Tobias was Mama's eldest brother. He was a bachelor and
had lived with the family all his life. As of right he verbally chastised
or spoiled the children depending on the circumstances.

Mama sighed and then looked up to see Aunt Margaret, her sister-
in-law, coming through the conservatory. She had arrived in time to
witness the end of the scene with Lantie and, as usual, her remarks
added fuel to the fire.

"That girl needs a firm hand or there will be no doing anything
with her. She is not too old to have a slipper round her bottom. I
would straighten her jacket for her if she were mine."

Aunt Margaret had no children of her own but this never inhibited
her from handing out advice to Mama or anyone else struggling to
rear their difficult young. On this occasion Mama was at a disadvantage

but decided not to go into details about the hubbub. She found herself making excuses for Lantie's bad behaviour.

"Of course she is at a funny age, just into her teens. She is very highly strung."

"Does she twang in a high wind?" enquired Than cheekily, poking his head round the door.

In exasperation Mama spun round and boxed his ears. "Either get off to Choir Practice or go up to bed," she stormed. Than disappeared in a trice.

Aunt Margaret arranged her ample frame in Poppa's large arm-chair.

Mama knew that she would have to wait until her sister-in-law was ready to reveal the purpose of her visit. Mama's other brother, Joshua, kept a thriving grocery business in Priors Ings and Aunt Margaret was the driving force behind the enterprise.

"Where's Tobias?" she asked when she had settled herself.

Uncle Tobias had taken refuge in the kitchen where he found comfort in his old Windsor chair away from the arguments and scoldings.

"He's in the kitchen, reading as usual," replied Mama. "Things look really bad don't they? Tobias says there will be a war quite soon. Jack agrees with him."

"Nonsense," sniffed Aunt Margaret. "Of course there won't be any war. Don't you remember what Mr. Chamberlain said on the wireless? 'Peace in our time' he said. It's all paper talk. They print anything to fill the pages. Just paper talk, that's what it is."

"Well, one or two lads from Priors Ings and Cowlswick have been called up," said Mama.

"They're Terriers. They always call up the Terriers for manoeuvres in the summer. But I haven't come to talk about the papers and war. Will you let Lantie come and help me in the shop next week? I am having the decorators in to do the sitting room and the front bedroom. I shall need to keep an eye on them and likely they will want cups of tea all day long to keep them going."

Mama started to speak but Aunt Margaret was in full flow and would not be interrupted.

"Lantie is quite sensible when it comes to helping in the shop. Though goodness knows what you will make of the girl. She is hopeless at sums and anything practical. As for using a needle, well, she might as well sew with a poker. Only the other week when she came to tea I set her to do a bit of hem stitching. A man on a galloping horse could have seen those stitches. Of course I made her take them out and do them again. All she thinks about is getting her nose in a book. She does too much reading. She will have eye strain if you don't watch out."

At last Mama managed to say her piece. "Jeanie is coming on Saturday. She is staying for the rest of the holidays. If you have Lantie you will have to have both of them." Here, Mama thought, she could see a solution to one of her problems.

"Oh no, not the two of them!" exclaimed Aunt Margaret. "I don't know why you encourage that friendship. Jeanie is far too chirpy and worldly wise for my liking. And as for that Cockney accent she puts on, well, words fail me."

Mama knew she was on high moral ground and made the most of it.

"Lantie and Jeanie have been friends since they were in the Infants Class. I hope the day will never come when I shall not welcome my children's friends to the house. I would much rather they brought their friends home than for them to be running wild goodness knows where."

Aunt Margaret had a beautiful and tidy home but she had few visitors. She worked hard to make the grocery business a success and her leisure time was sacrosanct.

"When one has a business house one cannot be forever entertaining," she remarked to Lantie on more than one occasion. "I am not like your Mama, who revels in having visitors. She has far too many to my way of thinking."

To placate her sister-in-law Mama put forward an idea.

14

"You could have Than to help you," she suggested. "He can be quite good most of the time and he is quick with mental arithmetic."

"No thank you," said Aunt Margaret hastily. "I'm not saying that he cannot be a help but he eats too much when he gives a hand. How that boy can eat! Sweets, currants, candied peel, bits of cheese, anything he fancies goes into his mouth. I don't mind him having a few sweets; I know all those open boxes are tempting but he never knows when to stop." She paused and then, in a conciliatory tone, she said, "You know, he has more about him than Lantie. He is quick, good at games and very talented at handwork. That was a fine dishcloth he knitted for me. Fancy them teaching boys to knit at school."

Mama forbore to tell her that Than's knitting skills were the results of his misbehaviour in the gardening class. Any boys who fooled about or slid off behind the potting shed to avoid the hard digging were sent back to school to join the girls in the needlework class.

Than and one or two other naughty boys regularly found themselves sitting at one end of a long bench. They were provided with thick wooden needles and dish-cloth cotton and were made to chant as they worked.

"In – over – under – off, in – over – under – off," at each stitch so that they had no chance to chatter or backslide. As a result Mama and Aunt Margaret had new dishcloths for which Mama paid twopence each.

"Never mind, I expect I shall manage," said Aunt Margaret. "I must go now as I have left a casserole in the oven for supper. Then I must do the accounts. One's work is never finished in business, you know."

She eased herself out of the armchair and prepared to leave. As she turned to go she looked out of the window into the front garden and saw Poppa coming up the path.

"Here's Jack coming home for his supper. Whatever is he carrying?" wondered Mama.

Aunt Margaret delayed her departure to find out.

15

Poppa came round the front of the house, past the greenhouse which clung to the side of it and entered through the door at the back. The conservatory was a long narrow structure of wood and glass. The wooden frame was made from an old rood screen which had been discarded from the church in the last century.

Mama and Aunt Margaret met him in the hallway and inspected his bundle which was wrapped in a piece of sacking. It was a small, young cat which was covered in oil.

"Get me some hot water and soap and old rags, please love," said Poppa. "This poor little thing had fallen into a barrel of oil in the garage when I found it. If I can wash off most of the oil it should be all right. Luckily its head didn't go under." Aunt Margaret was not very fond of cats so she took her leave. Mama dashed into the kitchen to put on a kettle of water. Then she fetched an old enamel bowl from the pantry and got out some clean rags from a drawer in the big kitchen dresser. Uncle Tobias, oblivious to the commotion, sat in his chair and continued reading.

Gently Poppa put the little cat on a towel on the draining board. Slowly and carefully he began to clean its fur with a rag and hot soapy water. "What about supper, love?" murmured Mama from time to time.

"Later, later," replied Poppa.

Eventually he cleaned every inch of the cat's fur; then he rinsed off the soap and dried its body with the towel. He gave it some bread and milk and settled it in a cardboard box which he had lined with old cloths. The little cat gazed up at him as if she knew he was her benefactor.

"There, little one, you'll feel better now," he said. "Goodness knows where it came from. I heard it meowing and found it in a barrel of oil."

Poppa had a garage on the outskirts of Priors Ings. It was only a few minutes walk down the lane from the Prior's House where the family lived. His small haulage and engineering business meant that he worked long and irregular hours. Nevertheless he was able to make a reasonable living in spite of the Thirties' slump.

16

Lantie came downstairs very quietly and stood beside Poppa as he cleared up after his ministrations. She avoided Mama's eye and said, "It's a pretty little thing. Can we keep it Poppa?"

"We have enough animals here with two cats and a dog," snapped Mama. "Who is going to feed it? Not you or Than I'll be bound."

Poppa sensed the tense atmosphere and, as usual, he tried to ease it.

"I think this little one is a stray. I'll ask around but I doubt if anyone will claim it. Perhaps we can give her a home. If you were to help with feeding the animals, I guess Mama would agree."

"Oh yes, I'll help," said Lantie eagerly. Mama sniffed and said nothing.

Poppa had his supper and they settled down in the sitting room. Uncle Tobias stayed in the kitchen, still reading.

Mama was somewhat mollified after Poppa had relaxed and related his day's activities. He enquired about her doings.

"Margaret came to ask if Lantie could go and help in the shop next week. I told her that Jeanie was coming to stay but she doesn't want both of them. She thinks they will giggle and be silly every time a customer comes in, so – – – – –"

"Poppa," interrupted Lantie. "Can we go pea-picking next week? Please, please."

Mama's pretty face flushed with anger.

"I've told her that they cannot go and there's an end to it! Pea-picking indeed! Think what they might see or hear! I said that you would forbid it."

Poppa paused to press some tobacco into the bowl of his pipe. He lit it and drew upon the stem before he spoke.

"You know, I think it might not be a bad idea. They will learn what manual labour means. As for seeing or hearing anything they shouldn't, most of the pea-pickers are respectable working women. The tramps who stay under the bridge are a decent lot of men. They want to work and would not use foul language in front of the womenfolk. I'm inclined to think it might be a good experience for them. Lantie is thirteen and Jeanie is fourteen and has just left school, so they are not little ones any more. Think about it, my love. It would get them out from under your feet during the day." He smiled at Mama and although she was not wholly placated she seldom gainsaid anything that Poppa suggested. She pursed her lips and said, "Well, I'll think about it. I'm not saying 'Yes' mind you. It will depend on how you behave in the next day or two."

Lantie flung herself at Poppa and hugged him. "Oh, thank you, Poppa, thank you. I will be good!" she said. Then, turning to Mama, "I'm sorry I shouted and slammed the door."

The following Saturday Lantie went to the bus stop in Beast Fair to meet her friend. Jeanie had spent most of her young life in Priors Ings. Her father had been a scholarly man who was gassed in the Great War. He had rented a property on the outskirts of the little town, a pretty house with orchards and some land. Here he hoped to establish a smallholding and improve his health in the fresh country air.

From a tiny hut at the end of a long drive he made a precarious living selling fruit, vegetables and eggs.

Jeanie's mother was a small, warm-hearted Cockney woman, generous to a fault. Her face was lined from the cares of bringing up a family in genteel, grinding poverty but she never lacked a smile and a welcome.

In spite of the pure air around Priors Ings Jeanie's father died in the late twenties. Her mother, with one daughter at a local grammar school and Jeanie at the nearby Church School, struggled to make a living for several more years. Lantie used to love going to Jeanie's house, aptly named, Mount Pleasant. Before Mama and Poppa and the family moved to the Prior's House they lived in a late Georgian property in Beast Fair. From there she could go out through the gate in the wall at the bottom of the garden and walk along the lane to the Tollington Road. She went past the Church School which her grandfather had built in the last century and came at last to the entrance of the drive to Jeanie's house. This meant she had another long walk past two orchards and a garden to the house itself. The land stretched beyond the buildings to the railway line.

The place was surrounded by farm land and was a lonely spot, had anyone been worried about such a thing. Winter and summer Jeanie and Lantie played in the orchards and old hen houses at Mount Pleasant. They learned to ride their fairy cycles, wobbling about and falling off and suffering many grazed knees, arms and legs.

Finally they succeeded in staying upright and balanced. Then they were able to race madly up and down the long drive.

Lantie preferred to play at Jeanie's house rather than at home, the supervision was more relaxed than under Mama's watchful eyes. They were able to climb trees and play noisy games without let or hindrance.

From time to time Mama insisted that they should play in her garden but they contrived to get away as much as possible.

In the summertime, Lantie had to be home by seven thirty and by six o'clock in the winter. On dark nights she would take a short cut along a yew-lined path in Jeanie's garden. This led across the meadows, along the back of the school playground and past a farmhouse. The journey in the dark did not trouble her, especially if it was a clear night. She would dawdle along and sometimes she sat on a stile between the meadows and gazed upwards, hoping to see a shooting star. It was all very quiet and peaceful except for the cows munching the sweet grass.

Through the wicket gate near the farm the path ran behind a high wall and into a 'ginnel' or 'snicket' as the passages in Priors Ings were called. Here she came out near the church and into the gas-lit High Street.

This was the part of the journey home which she disliked. Often there were gangs of noisy boys playing 'Tally Ho' or jostling each other under the street lamps. She kept close to the church wall, well away from them. Then she ran like the wind down Market Place and along the cobbles of Beast Fair to the safety of home.

Jeanie's mother struggled to make a living at Mount Pleasant as the Thirties slump deepened. Each summer she sat in the little hut at the end of the drive, trying to sell fruit, vegetables, flowers and honey. In the spring and early summer she went from door to door in Priors Ings with bunches of daffodils, primroses and violets. The garden and orchards became neglected and when Jeanie's older sister left the grammar school and went away to train as a nurse, she gave up the struggle. Jeanie and her mother packed up and 'flitted' as the locals termed it, to a mining district some fifteen miles away.

Lantie wept copiously when Jeanie left Priors Ings but the latter was philosophical about the move.

"It'll be a change, somefink different won't it? You gotta keep having a change else life gets dull, Ma says."

The two girls visited each other but they both missed the unkempt grounds of Mount Pleasant.

"Stop grumbling," said Mama crossly. "You have a garden here and an orchard and a stream."

"But the Prior's House isn't the same," moaned Lantie. What she meant was that it was too easy for Mama to come through the garden and into the orchard to see what they were doing. Climbing trees was not an activity that was encouraged. However, Jeanie kept coming and the girls enjoyed her visits to Priors Ings.

Lantie waited at the top of Beast Fair and when the green West Riding bus arrived Jeanie hopped off it.

"Wotcher, Lantie," she said cheerily.

"You've got a costume," breathed Lantie, enviously looking at the smart two piece suit which Jeanie was wearing. She was a slim fair girl and her pretty hair waved to her shoulders.

"Mama says I can't have a costume until I'm sixteen. That's years away," sighed Lantie.

"I gotta have one so I look smart when I go for a job. I ain't got one yet but I will have soon. Ma and me are going down to London to stay with her folks. There's lots of jobs in London. Wotcher got for dinner?"

Jeanie carried her suitcase and the two girls linked arms and ambled through the streets and down the lane to the Prior's House.

"Ma fitted me up with new clothes, undies an' all," said Jeanie. "She's paying the Tally man one and ninepence a week but she reckons it's worth it for me to get a good job."

Again Lantie sighed and envied Jeanie – lucky Jeanie who had left school and was going out into the world to make her fortune while she was stuck at the grammar school for years and years. Then, if Mama had her way, she had to train to be a teacher.

She brightened up at the thought of her news and eagerly told Jeanie of the plan to go pea picking.

"Have you brought any old clothes with you?" she asked.

"Course I have," retorted Jeanie. "I brought me oldest frocks, 'cos Ma said I wasn't to muck up me costume. Anyway she said if you shoved me in the stream again it wouldn't matter if I was wearing me old frock."

"I didn't push you in, you were running across the plank when you slipped and fell in," said Lantie indignantly.

"Yeah, I know, but I had to tell Ma and yer Mam, somefink din' I?"

Laughing they went through the back gate to the Prior's House and entered the conservatory, which everyone called the verandah. Mama welcomed Jeanie, admired her costume and then insisted she went upstairs and changed before she had lunch.

"It's a beautiful costume, isn't it? Mama can I ——"

"No," replied Mama, knowing full well what she wanted.

After their meal the two girls spent some time petting the new cat which was recovering from its ordeal in the oil barrel. Whenever it heard Poppa's voice it rushed to meet him and rubbed round his ankles. When he sat in his large armchair in the evening it climbed up and stretched itself round the back of his neck and lay like a fur collar across his shoulders.

Later in the afternoon the girls went into the orchard. They sat on a fallen tree to gossip and make plans for the coming weeks.

Having recovered from her chagrin over their proposed venture, Mama determined to make the best of it. She sewed two little bags and made drawstrings with cords to go round their necks. These were to hold any money they might earn.

At six thirty the following Monday morning Mama roused Lantie and Jeanie from their beds and when they had dressed and come downstairs she made them eat a cooked breakfast. Earlier she had cut sandwiches and buttered currant bread which she wrapped in greaseproof paper and packed into a cloth bag. To these items she added a bottle of Tizer and two old cups. These refreshments were known as 'drinkings' and would sustain them during the day.

Two old sunbonnets and two ancient coats lay on a chair.

"Oh, Mama! We shall look frights in those things," gasped Lantie in horror.

"Frights or not you will wear them. It is very cold first thing, even in the summer and if the sun gets out at midday you could both have sunstroke. Now you either wear them or stay at home, which is it to be?"

They walked to the Market Place and waited with a jovial crowd for the lorry to come and take them to the pea fields. There were some of the tramps who spent the summer under the viaduct of the bridge and many cheerful, laughing women with baskets and wooden stools.

"You fresh 'uns, are yer loves?" asked one plump matron. "Come on now, up yer get into t'lorry."

Lantie noted that the others were dressed in far more outlandish clothes than the ones she and Jeanie were wearing. The plump lady kindly showed them what to do when they got to the pea field.

"Now, sithee, me loves, get a sack an' put it at the end of your row. That's yer marker. Then, when you've pulled a pinnyful take it back to the sack and keep doing that until yer sack is full. Oh dear, you 'avent got pinnies on to put t'peas in. You'll have to pull the peas into the skirts of your frocks. Lift 'em up like this and mek a bag to hold t'peas."

"But we shall show our underwear," protested Lantie.

The woman guffawed. "Nay love, everybody'll be too busy to be looking at yer bloomers. Tomorrow you'd best wear a pinny, or bring a basket. It'll be easier for yer."

Jeanie and Lantie bent their backs and started pulling up the fronds out of the ground and plucking the peas. They found it difficult to hold their frocks and pull the peas at the same time. The peas they picked fell on the ground. The man on the weighing machine took pity on them and brought two old baskets for them to use.

When the baskets were full they carried them to the sacks at the start of the row and put the peas inside.

By the time everyone stopped for drinkings at one o'clock they had filled one bag each. The weighing machine man responded to the call of the girls' new friend.

"Ere, Bert. Come and lug these sacks over for these young lasses and weigh 'em."

He obeyed and after balancing the bags on the machine he heaved them to one side and handed them ninepence each. They put the money in the little purses which were hanging round their necks.

Thankfully they sat down under a tree in the hedgerow and ate their sandwiches and cake.

"Don't drink too much Tizer, Lantie," warned Jeanie, "else you'll keep wanting to go behind the hedge."

By the time the field was cleared they had picked only half a bag each.

"Put 'em together and mek a full bag," advised the weighing machine man.

This they did and he solemnly handed them fourpence halfpenny each.

The girls arrived back at the Prior's House about half past five, dirty, very tired and extremely hungry. Mama had prepared a hot meal for them, but she insisted that they had a bath before they ate.

During the afternoon she had filled the copper in the wash-house in the back garden and lit a fire under it. The only water in the Prior's House came from wells in the garden. Poppa had had bathroom fittings installed but, as there was no mains water, having a bath entailed a certain amount of hard work. When the water in the copper had boiled, it had to be carried in buckets from the wash-house, across the garden, through the conservatory and up the stairs to the bathroom.

"We'll both use the same water," said Jeanie. Lantie looked shocked.

23

"Oh, you can go first – I don't care," said her friend. "Cor, you ain't 'arf prim and proper, you are."

Poppa arrived home as the girls came downstairs and they were all able to have a meal together.

"And how much did the labourers in the field earn today?" he asked with a smile.

"One and three halfpence. We picked a bag and a half each. Oh, Poppa it was such hard work," said Lantie feelingly.

"So you won't be going tomorrow?" he teased.

"Oh yes we will," replied Jeanie. "It's hard work but it ain't going to put us off. We'll pick two bags tomorrow, you'll see." She turned to Mama,

"Can we have pinnies or a basket to pick in tomorrow, please?"

They were too tired to listen to the wireless, read, talk or argue with Than. By half past eight they were both in bed and sound asleep. The next morning Mama had to shake them hard to wake them up. They ate their breakfasts, gathered up their things and left the house still rubbing the sleep from their eyes.

The pea-pickers greeted Jeanie and Lantie like old friends.

"Got yer pinnies and drinkings, loves? Up yer get on t'lorry. Now 'utch up a bit an' give the rest of us some room."

On the second day they picked two bags of peas each. Although they were exhausted by the time they reached home they were exhilarated by their earning power.

"We earned one and sixpence each today, Mama."

After their baths and a meal the two wage earners fell asleep in the living room chairs. Mama woke them up to have cups of cocoa and biscuits, then she shooed them off to bed.

"They'll never last the week out at this rate," she opined to Poppa.

"I think they will," he smiled. "Didn't I say it would be good experience for them?"

By the end of the first week the girls had got into the routine of work. One lunch time they were sitting together in the shade of a hedge. They ate their sandwiches and wondered if they would ever manage to pull more than two bags of peas a day. Some of the pickers pulled six or even seven.

Suddenly Jeanie changed the conversation. "See that woman in the red skirt and white blouse? She's having a baby soon," she said knowledgably.

"The fat one in the green bonnet?" asked Lantie glancing along the side of the field. Jeanie was a quick-witted, noticing girl, unlike Lantie who was inclined to day dream. "How do you know?"

"Cos I know," replied Jeanie. "I can tell by looking at her. When she gets big enough the doctor will cut her open with a knife, right up to her belly button and let the baby out." Lantie looked at her in horror.

"Are you sure? Mama gave me two little books to read. They were about babies and things but they didn't say anything about knives."

"But it's true, honestly. I heard Ma and Aunt Em talking about somebody having a baby. An' the doctor cut her right open with a carving knife. Babies are begetted, you know. I read about it in the Bible. They were always begetting in the Bible. I've learnt everyfink I know from the Bible an' listening to Ma and Aunt Em."

Lantie was rendered speechless for a few moments but she was saved from having to reply as everyone started to pack up their belongings and go back to work.

The following week the pea pickers went further afield to crops in villages four or five miles from Priors Ings. At the end of each day, some of the women would glean peas to take home for their evening meal.

Jeanie's sharp eyes soon noticed something odd.

"D'you see how some of the women start to waddle at the end of the day?" she asked. Lantie hadn't noticed any such thing.

"Yes, an' do you know why? When they get towards the end of the field they start stuffing peas into their bloomers. An' that makes 'em waddle, see?"

"Why do they do that when they are allowed to glean after the field is cleared?" Lantie was puzzled.

"Cos only the small pods are left behind. So they put the big ones away while they are picking. You could fill your bloomers an' take some home for your Ma. I can't cost I'm wearing my cami-knickers."

"Oh, no," said Lantie, aghast. "Mama would be furious and maybe she wouldn't let us come again."

When they were on their way home on the Wednesday of the second week, Jeanie dropped her bombshell.

"I'm off home on Saturday. Shall we finish tomorrow an' have a day off on Friday? We could go for a walk or a long bike ride."

Lantie felt as if she had been struck a blow. "But I thought you were staying until the end of the school holidays?"

Mama echoed this sentiment when they got home.

"No! I'm off on Sat'dy. There's going to be a war an' I want to be with Ma and Aunt Em. We might go down to London to the East End an' stay with Ma's folks. I'll get a good job in London. Our Margy has gone nursing and Ma says there's nothing to keep us up North. It'll be real exciting living in London."

Lantie was very downcast on the next morning and during their last day in the peafields.

"What's up love? Lost half a crown an' found sixpence 'have yer?" asked one of the women.

"Cheer up, matey," said Jeanie. "We've had a lot of fun and earned some brass. Tomorrow we'll go to the chemist and buy a present for yer Ma."

"Why?" asked Lantie.

"Cor, you ain't 'arf ungrateful, ain't you? She's got up early every morning an' got our breakfast an' drinkings. She's given us Tizer an' lemonade an' cooked a good supper. I reckon she deserves a present." Jeanie sounded indignant.

"Yes, of course," agreed Lantie ashamed of her thoughtlessness. "What shall we buy her?"

"Some make-up," replied Jeanie promptly. "The Best! We'll get her some Yardley's face cream. Its in lovely jars with a sort of pink wasp on top. An' some Yardley's powder as well. Pity she doesn't wear lipstick. She'd look smashing in lipstick."

"Goodness, that's going to take most of what we've earned. Yardley's is ever so expensive. Mama always uses Pond's Vanishing Cream."

"Garn! We've done well and money's made to be spent. It ain't no good lying in the bank. You've gotta spend it an' enjoy it. My Ma never had any to spend but when I get a job I shall give her all she wants. I'll look after her proper."

They bade farewell to their fellow pea-pickers on the Thursday evening, Lantie a little sadly and Jeanie as chirpy as ever.

"Shall you go again when I've gone home?" asked Jeanie.

"No! It wouldn't be the same without you. It was hard work and fun but I shall never go again," she replied.

Mama was delighted with her make-up and hugged and kissed both of them. Poppa teased them gently and called them his little plutocrats. He would not tell them what he meant but bade them look it up in the dictionary.

"I'm going to be one of those one day," declared Jeanie, when they had discovered what a plutocrat was.

"No you won't 'cos you'll spend all your money as soon as you get it," retorted Lantie.

On the Saturday morning Jeanie packed away her holiday clothes and appeared once again in her costume and blouse. She had washed her hair with Mama's Drene shampoo the previous night and she looked very attractive. She thanked Mama and Poppa for a lovely holiday and said goodbye to Than and Uncle Tobias.

The two girls walked through Prior Ings to Beast Fair and waited until the bus appeared. They did not kiss or hug one another.

"Cheerio, Lantie, me old mate. See yer sometime," called Jeanie as she swung herself on to the platform of the double decker bus.

"Bye, Jeanie."

Lantie watched the bus until it was out of sight. She fought back her tears and walked slowly through Priors Ings to the Prior's House. She felt lonely and unhappy. She would have been devastated had she known then that she would never see or hear from Jeanie again.

CHAPTER 3

Autumn, 1939

The morning of Sunday, September 3rd 1939 was hot and sunny in Priors Ings. For one reason or another, nobody from the Prior's House had gone to church. Mama was busy preparing lunch in the kitchen whilst Poppa was clearing the shelves in the loft ready for storing the fruit crop from the orchard. Uncle Tobias had lined up a row of shoes on the old school bench in the conservatory and was cleaning them.

Suddenly the back garden gate was opened and Annie, who lived in the nearby gatehouse cottage, hurried to the door. She was a comely, well-made woman in her thirties. She was employed by the LMS Railway Company to open the big gates for horses and carts to cross the railway lines. Cows were brought from the fields in Gowhill Lane and taken over the crossing to the farm for milking.

Then they were taken back to the fields. This happened each morning and evening in the thirties. Annie worked seven days a week. For good measure she kept house for her father, a retired railwayman.

On this particular morning she was somewhat agitated,

"Have you heard the news?" she asked. "Mr Chamberlain's going to speak on the wireless at eleven o'clock. It sounds very serious."

Mama had gone out to the conservatory when she saw Annie appear. Poppa came down the loft ladder but it was Uncle Tobias who spoke.

"No, we haven't heard the news all weekend. The wireless accumulator's gone dead an' the other one's down at the Gas Works being charged up. One of those children should have fetched it home yesterday. There ought to be a different going-on in this house. They should be made to do as they're told. Dratted wireless! As dead as a doornail just when we need it!"

Gloomily Uncle Tobias returned to his task of cleaning shoes.

"Never mind," said Annie, "you can all come over and listen to our wireless." Turning to Poppa, she asked fearfully, "Does it mean there's going to be war?"

Poppa looked serious and nodded. "I reckon nothing can stop it now."

Lantie and Than became excited at the thought of a war, conjuring up as it did for them, pictures in their encyclopaedias and Poppa's stories of the Great War.

"Mama, will Poppa have to go to the war? Will he go back to Flanders?"

"He will not," replied Mama. "He'll be far too old this time, thank God. Now stop asking silly questions. Nobody knows what's going to happen until the Prime Minister speaks."

Later on that morning they trooped into Annie's bright, spotless living room and waited for the stroke of eleven. Uncle Tobias refused to go on the principle that they should have been able to listen to the news on their own wireless.

At eleven o'clock Big Ben boomed out and they all fell silent.

They listened to Neville Chamberlain making the broadcast that would change the lives of millions.

"They were wrong, weren't they lad?" remarked Annie's father to Poppa. "They told us that the Great War would be the war to end all wars. Twenty years on and now they're at it again. I'm glad that I'm an old man. I shan't see the end of this one."

When they emerged from the cottage into the warm September sunshine, Lantie thought how strange it was that anyone should declare war on such a beautiful day. They went back to the Prior's House and acquainted Uncle Tobias with the news.

"I could have told you that. The papers have been full of it for weeks," was his reply.

Mama made cups of Camp Coffee and they sat in the kitchen and talked for a long time.

"It won't be like the last one," said Poppa. "It is to be hoped not," replied Mama. "All those terrible casualties and the telegrams that kept coming and coming. No wonder people still dread the sight of a telegram to this day." She explained to Lantie and Than, how during the Great War, news of a loved one's death was conveyed by way of a telegram. Many years later Lantie met an old lady who told her that the telegraph boy came five times to her home between 1915 and 1918.

"There were eight of us children in the family and now only the girls are left," she said.

"This time, things could be much worse. They could bomb towns and cities and the civilians will be in the front line as well as the troops," remarked Poppa. He began to reminisce about life in France and got out his medals which usually appeared only on Armistice Day. The children examined them and listened as he identified each one.

That reminded Mama of one of her own memories. She riffled through a drawer in the sideboard and brought out a small oval photograph of herself. It was taken when she was seventeen years old and had just put up her hair. She looked a beautiful young girl.

She explained how she had given the photograph to a young man

30

in Priors Ings who was going to France. He had asked her to write to him. Several letters passed between them and in late 1915, the young man's parents had a telegram with news of his death.

Shortly after this sad event, Mama received an envelope written in a strange hand. Enclosed was her photograph and a letter from an Australian soldier. He told her how he had picked up her photograph on the battlefield and, as her name and address were on the back, he was returning it. The young Australian asked her to write to him, which she did. She ended the story by saying sadly, "When one of my letters was returned I knew that he too had been killed. Oh, the slaughter was terrible. All those young lives lost and now it seems as if it was all for nothing."

The morning after the day war was declared, when Poppa and Uncle Tobias had gone to work, Than was despatched with the offending accumulator and sixpence to collect the recharged one from the local gas works. When he returned he fixed it into the back of the wireless and communications with the outside world were restored.

At nine o'clock Phoebe arrived. Years ago she had come to the family as a nursemaid when Lantie was a baby. She stayed on to help Mama about the house and in the late thirties she was still coming each morning from Monday to Friday to 'tidy-up' and do various unspecified tasks. Mama and Lantie were very attached to Phoebe and she was as much involved in the lives of the family at the Prior's House as with those of her own elderly parents.

Little work was done that morning. As they sat and drank coffee, they talked about the news and speculated on the future.

"I don't expect it will make much difference to us," said Mama. "Jack and Tobias are too old and Than is too young to go to war. I expect we shall have food rationing but we had that the last time. No! I suppose life will carry on as usual."

If Mama and Phoebe could have looked down the years ahead, the former would have been very disturbed and the latter pleasantly surprised.

Within a few months Phoebe had left the Prior's House, having

31

been directed by the Authorities into war work. As she had elderly parents she was posted near to home so that she could remain with them.

Later in the war a man from one of the ministries was billeted with Phoebe's family, where he stayed for the duration. He was older than Phoebe, a well spoken, well educated townsman. At the end of the war, to the surprise of many in Priors Ings, they were married and went to Rome for a honeymoon.

By that time Mama knew that her dear, faithful Phoebe would never come back to the Prior's House. When, in her late thirties, Phoebe produced a beautiful daughter, Mama was torn between rejoicing at such happiness and sadness at her own loss. All this lay in the future. On that September day life seemed set to continue on its even tenor.

"Shall we be going on holiday?" asked Lantie. "Of course not, people don't go away on holiday when there's a war on," scolded Mama.

Lantie had a particular reason for asking about holidays. In September the previous year, Phoebe had been invited to stay with relations in Scarborough. She had asked Mama and Poppa if she could take Lantie with her. The family had already been on holiday in Surrey. They stayed with Poppa's kinsfolk; 'Going down Home' was how he fondly referred to visits to his native county. After some discussion it was decided that Lantie could go with Phoebe who was so sensible and reliable.

Once they were in Scarborough, Phoebe and Lantie were more like two young people of the same age. Lantie, away from home, became more grown up and Phoebe, away from her loving but strict parents, became younger and carefree.

It was a happy holiday which neither of them ever forgot. They climbed the hill to the castle, and walked in the Valley Gardens. They took trips on the pleasure boats out into the bay. In the evenings, after supper, they would go down into the town to admire the displays of coloured lights. One night they went to the Open Air Theatre to see *Tannhauser*. Phoebe's cousin kindly lent them rugs and hot water bottles, for the night air was chilly and the performance did not start until after dark.

One of the highlights of their week was when they went to a cricket match at the Scarborough Cricket Festival. There they saw the great Don Bradman at the wicket. On another occasion they went to the pictures and saw *Snow White and the Seven Dwarfs*. Both were overawed by the huge cinema and the giant screen, so unlike the local picture houses in towns near Prior Ings.

"Wasn't that a marvellous holiday last year, Phoebe? It was the very best holiday I've ever had," enthused Lantie.

Mama looked hurt, "You've been on some lovely holidays with us, to Scarborough and lots of other places."

Lantie was not old enough to realise it was the freedom of being away from their families that made it so special for both of them.

"Never mind, we'll go again one day, when the war is over," soothed Phoebe, but of course they never did.

Later that week one of Than's special friends, Albert, came for the day. His parents and Mama and Poppa had been friends for many years. They lived about eight miles away and the families often exchanged visits.

Albert came on the bus. He was a tall, well made boy of twelve. Once he had arrived at the Prior's House in some distress as the bus conductor would not believe that he was under fourteen years old and had charged him the adult fare. Mama waxed indignant on his behalf and insisted on refunding him the difference.

Albert and Will, Than's other great friend, went to the same public school. The three boys spent a lot of time together on Will's father's farm. Sometimes they went for long bicycle rides or roamed the woods and fields looking for mushrooms and birds' nests.

On this visit Albert sat in the kitchen and related the family news.

"Dad's taking Mother and the girls to Leeds on Saturday to rig them out with clothes and underwear, and things. He says there will be clothes rationing before long."

Mama pondered over this bit of information and made a mental note to tell Poppa when he came home that evening.

Will and Than initiated Albert into some of the mischievous ways of the boys of Priors Ings. They crept into the Clog Mill when it was deserted at lunch time. Risking life and limb they would set the conveyor belt going so that they could ride along it.

One farmer had some very fine apples in his orchard. Regardless of the fact that he had plenty of fruit at home, Than volunteered to climb over the wall and get some of the lovely ones hanging on the low branches. He was busily throwing apples over to his friends when the orchard's owner came up behind him. He seized Than by the scruff of his neck. "Nah then, yer young divil. Pinchin' my apples eh! Coom 'ere an' I'll skelp yer backside." By dint of much struggling Than managed to free himself from the farmer's grasp. He dodged between the trees and leapt over a gate before he could be caught again.

It was accepted by the boys that if they were caught scrumping they would get a good clout or a skelping. All knew that it was no use going home to complain because they would be likely to qualify for another walloping from angry parents. Occasionally Poppa caught boys in his orchard. In his quiet manner he would ask them to show him where they got in. They would lead him to a hole in the hedge. Then he bade them go through it and as they did so he assisted them with the toe of his boot on their backsides.

At the corner of Mill Street and Railway Street in Priors Ings was a small general store kept by a kindly old man who, for some obscure reason was nicknamed 'Bunkum'. He had much to contend with from the local youths. Older boys would send younger ones into the shop to ask for such commodities as pigeon's milk toffee, a wool riddle or half a pound of elbow grease.

Empty lemonade bottles qualified for a penny return deposit on each one. Oftimes the old man would say, "Leave the bottles by the door lads, ready for the delivery man." The accumulation of bottles led to boys going into the shop, picking up a couple of empty bottles and carrying them to the counter. By the time old Bunkum had plodded into the shop, the boys were waiting innocently for their tuppence refund. It was a long while before he realised what was happening and moved the bottles to the far side of his counter. Thus the boys filled the long summer days of the school holidays.

After the declaration of war changes came faster to Priors Ings than most people had expected. Gas masks were distributed and caused many misgivings and objections from the older members of the community.

"I'll die afore I'll put that thing on," declared Uncle Tobias, and this sentiment was echoed by many of his contemporaries.

Local lads were called up and khaki clad strangers filled the streets. The Town Institute, a long low depressing building, was turned into a Forces Canteen. Mama and a number of ladies joined the Women's Voluntary Service and took turns to serve tea, coffee and sandwiches to the soldiers.

The Clog Mill buzzer no longer signalled the end of the workers' lunch break at one o'clock each day. Its plaintive sound was reserved for Air Raid Warnings and the All Clear. Everyone expected immediate air attacks even though, at the time, there were no obvious targets in the area.

While Mama was busy lining curtains to comply with the blackout regulations, Poppa and Annie's father started to construct an air raid shelter in the orchard. It was very hard work, and as they dug down the roots of trees kept getting in the way. When they had cleared a rectangle of several feet deep and six or seven feet square, they lined the sides with old railway sleepers to stop the earth from falling in. They made seats on three sides and used old blocks of wood to form steps down into the shelter. The roof was made of corrugated iron sheets and they filled sacks with soil they had excavated and put them on top.

At last when all was finished, they stood back and looked at their handiwork. Poppa went down the steps at the entrance, ducked his head and went inside. It felt cold and damp even though the sun was shining outside.

"Well, lad, it's done! But I tell thee, I hope I never have to use it," said Annie's father. "So do I, so do I," replied Poppa fervently.

Early one morning Mama set off for the Town Institute, having given Lantie instructions to see about the lunch. It was the day that the first wave of evacuees was due to arrive. The Billeting Officers were present but it was the ladies of the town who provided refreshments and comfort for the incomers. They found themselves surrounded by a milling horde of frightened mothers, noisy children and howling babies. Priors Ings had never seen anything like the chaos in the Institute that day.

Mama rushed home at lunch time, full of horror and indignation.

"No, no! I couldn't eat a mouthful. Poor things! Most of them have only the clothes they are wearing and some of those children are alive with lice and fleas. Ask Uncle Tobias to fill the copper and get the water hot as soon as he comes home. And look for that fine tooth comb that I bought when you caught nits that time when you were in the First Form. I shall need a bath and a good combing of my hair when I get back."

Mama gave more instructions to Lantie and hurried out, saying, "I must get off as soon as possible. We shall have to have some here you know. You can take that sulky look off your face. I'll try and pick out a couple of clean ones."

Later in the day she arrived home with the evacuees she had chosen. They were two clean but unhappy looking mothers each carrying a baby. Mama did her best to make them feel wanted, offering baths and a hot meal. They refused the former and ate the latter without enthusiasm. The two women were quiet and subdued all evening and when they went upstairs to put their infants to bed they retired for the night.

Mama was flustered by their behaviour but she excused it saying, "Of course, they are tired and upset. They'll soon settle down. We must all try and make them feel welcome."

This remark was addressed to Lantie, who had had plenty to say at being turned out of the big front bedroom. She had spent months coaxing and persuading Uncle Tobias to move into her little room overlooking the fields and the river. Now that she had distributed all her books and possessions in her new quarters, she had to move again.

The following morning, Mama took cups of tea upstairs for her visitors. In reply to her query as to whether they had slept well, one looked glum and the other burst into tears. The two babies grizzled in their cots.

"We're off home this morning, Missus," said the glum one. "We can't stand it here any longer."

Mama flushed and prepared to be affronted.

"It ain't your fault, Missus. It's this horrible quiet, it gets on yer nerves. We'd rather go home an' risk the bombs than stop here. All this quiet gives you the horrors, it does. An' that graveyard across there is real creepy. Anyway, we're off home, bombs or no bombs."

After breakfast, in spite of Mama's protests they gathered up their babies and few possessions and went to catch a train back to the city.

Priors Ings had a constant stream of evacuees through the town during the first few months of the war. The deceptive quiet of the early hostilities lured many of them back to their own homes. Some remained, their stay lengthening from weeks to months and on into years. Some made lifelong friends and returned to visit their foster families decades after the war had ended.

Mama, whose hospitality was boundless, was not very fortunate with her evacuees. From the second wave she chose a young girl about ten years old. She was a bright, well-spoken child and Mama became very fond of her, treating her as a second daughter. She was given pocket money and became one of the family.

After several months the child was reclaimed by her parents. They appeared on the doorstep of the Prior's House one day and announced that they were taking her home. It transpired that the authorities had notified them that they must pay ten shillings a week towards her keep. This they considered outrageous.

Mama was very upset to see the child go. The heavy bombing of the cities had begun and the war was on in earnest. She begged the parents to reconsider their decision but they were adamant. Even Than was sorry to say goodbye to the little girl. Though they had been involved in many a quarrel, they were good friends. Only Lantie rejoiced at her departure. She was elated by the thought that she would no longer have to share her bedroom with anyone. Her joy was dimmed somewhat by the fact that Mama gave Lantie's second best coat, two dresses and her roller skates to the weeping child as she left the Prior's House for the last time.

As in the rest of the country, the blackout was strictly enforced in Priors Ings. Heavy lined curtains covered the windows and Poppa made a frame for the pantry window, so that no chink of light escaped into the lane. They stocked up with candles, flashlights and batteries. It had always been dark in autumn and winter around the Prior's House as it was outside the little town. Yet, from the conservatory, they used to look out and see the gaslamp shining at the top of Church Lane. Now the street lights were turned off and the darkness was total.

The huge Priory Church could not be blacked out so the evening services were held in the afternoon during 'Back End' and at the usual times in summer. The Harvest Festival of 1939 was its usual spectacular display. Mama decorated the font, which was her special area, with autumn flowers and foliage. She supplied some of the apples and pears which nestled amongst the corn and greenery on the window ledges.

The land had been ploughed and sown in the old way and the abundance of produce in the church assured everyone that all was safely gathered in. The Pie and Peas supper was held in the Old Grammar School, a low building dating from the 17th century in the corner of the churchyard. Everyone was lulled into a feeling of security.

November the fourth was the next highlight in the Priors Ings calendar, it being known as Mischief Night. This presumably commemorated the night when the Gunpowder Plotters gathered to finalise their plans. No one knew how long the custom of Mischief Night had been followed in Priors Ings. Very old men remembered their fathers and grandfathers talking about their exploits.

It was the one night when Mama forbade Than to cross over the doorstep. Be it Choir Practice or any other excuse, he was obliged to remain indoors lest he be led astray by other naughty boys bent on mischief. There was no malice in the tricks that the lads of Priors Ings played upon their neighbours and friends. They would knock on doors or ring bells and then run away. Sometimes they tied door knobs together with strong twine stretched across a street. Having knocked on both doors they retreated to a safe distance to watch the results. Garden gates were lifted off their hinges and placed alongside hedges. Bonfire guys were taken down and set up in front gardens to shock the household inhabitants when they drew back their curtains the next morning.

There was nothing menacing or vicious about the tricks. No old people felt threatened as they do with the Trick or Treat demands of present day Hallowe'en Night. The tricks were accepted with benign tolerance. The darkness of the blackout in 1939 lent an extra spice to the adventures of those who were allowed to go into the streets.

Bonfire Night on the fifth was cancelled for the duration of the war. This was a relief to Mama and Lantie as neither of them enjoyed the noise of the rockets, Jumping Jacks and other crackers. They used to watch from the sitting room window, while Poppa lit a bonfire in the orchard for Than and his friends. The boys were not allowed to touch the fireworks but the noisier they were the more they enjoyed them.

Poppa kept the Catherine Wheels until the end. These he fixed on the trees and he tried to set them going altogether so that they made a little display for the watchers in the house.

Afterwards they all trooped indoors for cocoa and Mama's treacle toffee, parkin pigs and, for some reason, pink and white coconut ice. Uncle Tobias ignored the whole proceedings and shut himself and the animals in the kitchen, where he read to his heart's content.

Food was still in reasonable supply for the first Bonfire Night of the war, so cocoa and refreshments were handed out as usual. Poppa managed to get some sparklers and indoor fireworks which could be set off on a board on the living room table. These sent up a small shower of stars but died down in seconds. Everyone agreed that it was not the same. The nights of the parkin pigs and Jumping Jacks, the guy, the bonfire and Catherine Wheels were gone for ever. After the war the children had other interests and the Prior's House and the orchard passed Guy Fawkes Night in quietness and shadows.

CHAPTER 4

Christmas

Every year, long before Stir-up Sunday in November, Mama began the Christmas preparations. The year 1939 was no exception. On Bank Holiday Monday at the beginning of August, a large section of the population of Priors Ings went on the Sunday School trip to Cleethorpes. On the Thursday of that week a smaller contingent went on the Choir trip across the Pennines to spend a day in Blackpool. When these events were over Mama started to collect her ingredients for the Christmas puddings and cakes.

As usual one pudding had been kept from the previous year and fed with brandy from time to time, so that it would be well matured. This was reserved for Christmas Day. The rest were made in a large earthenware bowl. Dried fruit, brown sugar, suet which was bought in a large piece from Butcher John's shop in Market Place, were

41

gathered together ready for the mixing. Apples from the orchard and eggs from the hens which Poppa kept in the field opposite the garden, were set aside. On pudding mixing day, the brandy which was used mainly as a restorative when any adult became poorly, was brought out from the back of the sideboard cupboard.

The apples and suet were grated and all the ingredients were put into the bowl and mixed with several eggs and a generous helping of brandy. Lantie and Than stirred the mixture and each made a wish, as did Mama. Even Poppa was persuaded to move the spoon around in the mixture and wish. Only Uncle Tobias scorned the practice saying, "Wishing never altered nowt."

The pudding bowls were greased and filled with the rich mixture. Usually Mama made six puddings: one to be kept for the following year; three to be eaten during the Festive Season or winter and two to be given away. Aunt Harriet received one of the extra puddings. She was the widow of one of Mama's brothers. She had two teenage children and she taught the Infants Class at the Church School in Priors Ings.

"Aunt Harriet hasn't the time to make puddings and cakes," explained Mama, when Lantie wanted to know why she gave away the extra ones. Aunt Harriet accepted it gratefully but Mama would not have dared to offer either puddings or cakes to Aunt Margaret. She made her own and would have been affronted at the thought that she did not do her duty in such matters.

Mama covered the pudding bowls with greaseproof paper and then placed cotton covers over the top. These she made from old pillow cases. They had draw strings so that they could be pulled tightly over the bowls. Each one had a handle which was stitched across the middle of the circle of cloth. These handles made it easy to lift the bowls out of the water after they had boiled for hours in the wash house copper.

When they were old, Than and Lantie would say to each other, "Nobody ever made such plum puddings as Mama, did they?" Than was of the opinion that she muttered a witch's spell over them as they bubbled in the copper. Than's wife, Marian, and Lantie used

Mama's recipe for many years but they never achieved the same results and the puddings never tasted so good.

By the time war was declared Mama's puddings were on the shelf and she had started making mincemeat. Dried fruit, butter, sugar and eggs were still plentiful that September and Mama made the most of them.

When she made her Christmas cakes one of the children was recruited as Assistant. There were one or two perks which went with this job so neither of them objected to helping. The candied lemon peel came in halves and still had the sugar in the hollows. Mama eased out the latter before she chopped up the peel. The helper made short work of the sugar.

She arranged all the ingredients on plates and dishes and spread them on the kitchen table. Plump raisins, that had been soaked overnight in sherry or spirits, sat alongside glacé cherries and other dried fruits. Only best farm butter and demerara sugar would do for the creaming. When the eggs were called for the Assistant had to break them one at a time on to a saucer. Mama smelled each egg to make sure that it was fresh before she put it into the mixture. Then the other items were added in turn.

"Flour! Ground almonds! Fruit!" Mama would call out and the appropriate plate or dish would be passed across the table. When everything had been mixed to her satisfaction, she would fill the cake tins which had been lined with greaseproof paper. Then who- ever was helping was allowed to scrape out the bowl and lick the wooden spoon which had been used for mixing. The word 'Salmo- nella' was not bandied about a great deal in Priors Ings in the thirties. No harm ever came to the bowl scrapers and spoon lickers.

The cakes, having been cooked in the coal-fired oven for several hours, were cooled and wrapped in layers of greaseproof paper. They were stored in empty biscuit tins. Into each tin, Mama would put a small apple, which was supposed to help to keep the cake moist. From time to time, the cakes were unwrapped and given a feed of sherry or whisky or whatever liquor was to hand.

The Christmas pig which Poppa kept with a farmer's pigs in a nearby village was killed in November. It was delivered to the house cut up into manageable pieces of hams, sides and legs, down to the meat for sausages and brawn. This largesse was salted, hung and shared among relations and friends. The first November of the war was the last time such abundance came to the Prior's House. It became illegal to kill a pig without a licence and the farmers were obliged to send all their produce to provide meat for the food rationing.

Poppa loved Christmas and he enjoyed all the preparations as well as the Festival itself. On Christmas Eve he and Mama would go to the Midnight Service in the old church. Lantie and Than were allowed to stay up with Uncle Tobias once they had solved the mystery of Father Christmas. When their parents came home from church there were Christmas drinks for everyone. Poppa would tease the children by wanting to open his presents before he went to bed.

"No, no, Poppa! You know we never, ever, open anything until after breakfast on Christmas morning!" they would chorus at him.

Christmas Eve was always a busy time for Mama. She prepared the vegetables and made the stuffing, which she spooned into the goose or turkey. The bird was put into the oven very early on Christmas morning after she came back from church. It cooked slowly for hours so that it was tender and ready for eating by lunchtime. There was no Midnight Service for Christmas in 1939. Instead they all went to the eight o'clock communion on Christmas morning.

Not many carol singers came to the Prior's House, which stood outside the little town. There were no street lamps to light them to the front or back gates. If children came on Christmas morning Poppa would give generously from a pile of pennies he had put on the kitchen mantelpiece. Albeit he refused to be fobbed off with a few gabbled bars of music. He insisted on hearing at least two verses of 'Once in Royal David's City' or whatever carol was being rendered, before handing over the money.

Frequently the postman came on Christmas morning with last minute cards or parcels. He was given a Christmas Box of half a crown, a reward for his faithful service throughout the year. The paper man, who had to cycle from Gowhill in all weathers to deliver the papers round Priors Ings, received the same amount. The dustmen, who came only once a week, were given two shillings.

Mama did not care for a lot of Christmas decorations. She displayed the numerous cards on mantelpieces and surfaces in the dining and sitting rooms. A couple of seasonal plaques were put over the mirrors and some holly was placed behind the pictures. Bowls of evergreens with two or three large chrysanthemums from the greenhouse would stand on the piano and sideboard.

When Lantie and Than were small, they made paper chains which they were encouraged to put up in the kitchen or their bedrooms. There was always a Christmas tree in the bay window of the sitting room. It was decorated with many baubles and lights. By the time it had shed its needles through to Twelfth Night, Mama would declare that it would be the very last one ever. Each year she was over-persuaded and another tree appeared until they became more and more difficult to obtain as the war continued.

Christmas dinner was a family affair with the five of them – Mama, Poppa, Uncle Tobias and the children – sitting down to eat at one o'clock. Afterwards Poppa washed the dishes, a feat which cause much hilarity as he was not a domesticated man. Then they all gathered around the wireless to listen to the King's Speech at three o'clock.

Occasionally, in the thirties, the family had gone down to Poppa's old home in Surrey to spend Christmas with his family. Being winter time, it was deemed too far to travel by car. They went by train and crossed London on the Underground to Waterloo. There they took another train which was followed by a bus journey and a long walk.

One year they arrived very late on Christmas Eve at the village in the depths of Surrey. From thence they had to walk more than a mile to the hamlet where grandpa's cottage stood. Poppa and Uncle Tobias, carrying heavy cases, led the way along the quiet country road while Mama trailed behind with the two tired children. Fretfully they cried, "Will Father Christmas have been before we get there? Will he have gone?"

"He will if you don't be quiet and behave," retorted Mama, who was in a state of exhaustion. "He only waits for good children."

Christmas of 1932 found the family at the cottage in Surrey. After Christmas dinner everyone gathered round the wireless for a notable occasion. The King himself, George V was to speak to the nation. They sat entranced at the sound of the gruff old voice of their monarch, speaking to them, the ordinary people of England. When he had finished, grandpa, then a very old man, got to his feet and raised his glass.

"The King! God Bless Him." All the adults and children stood up and followed his example. Even the little ones raised their glasses of orangeade and all repeated the words, "The King! God Bless Him."

In spite of the economic hardship of the Thirties, the majority of the ordinary people were staunch in their loyalty to their King and Country. Even a few years later such feelings remained strong in spite of the turbulence of the Abdication. Lantie was scolded roundly by Mama and Aunt Margaret for singing a verse she had heard in the school playground:

> "Hark, the Herald Angels sing,
> Mrs Simpson's pinched our King."

At home in the Prior's House, Christmas afternoon was Mama's high point. All the family and one or two friends came to high tea. Aunt Harriet, thin and prematurely aged with the strain of her full-time teaching post and bringing up a family, relaxed with her two children. Uncle Joshua and Aunt Margaret came, the latter and Mama having put aside their little differences for the Festive Season. Uncle Tobias was persuaded to put on his best suit and join the company. He did so only on condition that he could retire to the kitchen with his books and papers after the meal.

That first Christmas of the war, the table was lengthened by two extra sections. The white cloth was decorated with red and green crepe paper and white linen table napkins rested on each side plate. The usual delicacies were set out down the length of the table. There was home cooked ham, brawn and cold turkey, Mama's hand raised. Hot-water pastry pork pies were admired and tasted as good as they looked. Salads, chutneys and pickles accompanied the meats. On the sideboard trifles, jellies, sponges, small iced cakes and mince pies waited to be transferred to the table.

Everyone had to have a small present at teatime and Mama loved to think of different ways in which these could be presented. One year she make a huge snowball out of hoops and cotton wool. Inside it the presents were disguised as little snowballs. This had pride of place in the centre of the table. On another occasion she filled a large tureen full of little packages. Each parcel had a ribbon attached to it and the ribbons led to the plates. In 1939 the centrepiece was a huge home-made cracker with little crackers inside it. For many years Mama prided herself that the presents cost no more than a shilling each. It was only after the war broke out that she had to adjust her budget to accommodate rising prices.

After the meal everyone except Uncle Tobias adjourned to the sitting room to seat themselves amid boxes of dates and chocolates, bowls of nuts and candied fruits. The Christmas cake was displayed on a side table and was cut later in the evening. Slices were handed round on plates along with glasses of sherry or port wine.

After much talking and laughter someone, usually Uncle Joshua or Aunt Margaret, would play the piano. Christmas carols were sung and then a repertoire of old choruses going back to the Great War. 'Tipperary' and 'Keep the Home Fires Burning' were Poppa's favourites and were followed by 'Pack up your troubles' and 'Keep right on to the end of the Road'. Poppa also liked 'Sally' to be sung in honour of Mama. Some modern songs such as 'The Isle of Capri,' 'Roll along Covered Wagon' and 'Red Sails in the Sunset' were included to please the younger ones in the party.

On Boxing Day everyone went to Aunt Margaret's for tea. Here the food was just as lavish and was arranged with great care. There were more little presents but these were placed decorously on the side plates. Mama praised everything and a happy and peaceful time followed.

Aunt Margaret had dabs of brandy butter on her mince pies and offered slices of cheese with her Christmas cake. "It is a good old Yorkshire custom," she said without fail each year. Mama would never follow this practice as Poppa not only could never eat cheese but could not bear it to be near him when he sat at table. Years ago, when he was a boy, someone had shown him a piece of gorgonzola under a microscope. The sight of the live organisms in this morsel had given him a lifelong aversion to all cheeses.

There was more feasting and singing and consuming of Christmas cake, wine, nuts and chocolates at Aunt Margaret's house before the party broke up and everyone set out to walk home. At the end of Boxing Day Mama invariably remarked, "Well, Christmas is as far away as ever."

The following day much of the festive spirit had evaporated and routine took over. This involved the children sitting at the dining room table and writing their Thank You letters. Mama would brook no arguments.

"Get them done now or they will be hanging over your heads all the holidays. Neither of you will leave this room until those letters are written." The epistles were short and to the point but they were done in record time.

1939 was the very last Christmas when there was such a lavish display of food and presents at Prior's House. Throughout the war years and the long period of austerity that followed them Mama managed to make a semblance of bygone feasts. She hoarded rations, exchanged eggs and apples for other commodities and put on a brave show. The little teatime presents were often handmade but still presented in novel ways. During the war the Christmas and Boxing Day gatherings were augmented by soldiers whom the family befriended. The same traditions were observed but the war changed the celebrations at Prior's House for ever.

48

CHAPTER 5

A Quiet War

The winter of 1940 was a bitterly cold one. As in most dwellings in Priors Ings, central heating was non-existent in the Prior's House. Fires, extra blankets and hot water bottles were the time-honoured means of keeping warm. Every morning when the blackout curtains were drawn wonderful frost patterns were revealed on the bedroom windows. These beautiful pictures were no incentive for anyone to get out of bed, except Uncle Tobias. He seemed impervious to frost and snow and the war had given him a new lease of life.

In 1939 Tobias had gloomily contemplated retirement. He was over sixty-five years of age and he could have drawn the ten shillings a week Old Age Pension. Work had been scarce in the building trade in the thirties and he had spent as much time at home as in employment. Soon after the outbreak of war he discovered that there were jobs aplenty going and his age was no barrier. He arose each morning at five thirty and lit the kitchen fire. Mama came downstairs at six o'clock to get him his breakfast and pack his lunch. Then he went happily down the lane, sometimes whistling softly to himself, to catch a workman's train to wherever his skills were needed.

By 1940 life had changed for Poppa too. He left his garage at the end of the lane and took a job in an Ordnance Depot which had been set up about five miles from Priors Ings. He cycled to work every day and the hours were long. Often he had to go in on Saturdays and even Sundays if there was a sudden call for ammunition. Poppa used to get very tired but, ever philosophical, he assured Mama that the cycling kept him fit. The pay was not high but it was regular and he felt that it was far better to be employed close to home than to be directed into war work many miles away.

Poppa left the house each morning at seven o'clock and then Mama braced herself to get the children up and ready for school. They were both reluctant risers and she had to scold and cajole them before they would leave their beds. They had to catch the eight fifteen train to a town, some seven miles away, where they attended the local grammar school. Poppa used to tease Lantie and call her 'Last Minute Lizzie' for she was never on time no matter what the occasion. Yet, she was able to point out that, unlike Than, she never missed the train for school. In spite of Mama's threats and entreaties, he made many a last minute dash down the lane to the station, with his school satchel on his shoulder, his cap in one hand and a slice of toast in the other.

Phoebe no longer came to the Prior's house, having been conscripted for war work, and Mama had to cope with the housework as best she could. In addition she found herself encumbered with an unexpected chore. Poppa rented a field across the lane from the orchard. Here he kept a few hens whose efforts supplied the family with eggs. When rationing was introduced, anyone with more than thirty hens was obliged to register their fowls and send the eggs to the packing station. Poppa's hens were few in number and did not need to be officially recognised. On the other hand, they did not qualify for a ration of meal and had to rely on household scraps for their food.

With Poppa and Uncle Tobias away from the house for long hours and the children at school, it fell to Mama to feed the poultry. Although she was unused to hard work, she tackled the job with vigour. She boiled potato peelings and vegetable scraps in a big old pan on the kitchen fire. She mixed them with odds and ends of crusts and left over food and a good helping of spent hops. The latter were obtained from the local brewery at Cowlswick. Than or Uncle Tobias went each Saturday with a wheelbarrow to fetch them. Whether there was much goodness left in the hops after brewing was debatable.

During that cold winter Mama carried out her task without faltering. She swathed herself in a long, old overcoat belonging to Uncle Tobias and wound a huge scarf round her head and shoulders. Putting on a pair of Wellington boots she plodded down the lane and across to the field, balancing a bucket of food in one hand and a bucket of water in the other. Sometimes she had to return to get a spade to shovel a pathway in the snow from the field gate to the hen house. She performed this feeding routine twice a day from Monday to Friday. At the weekends Poppa, Uncle Tobias or Than took over the work.

Annie's elderly father, who was bed-ridden by early 1940 used to look out of his bedroom window and watch Mama's comings and goings.

"My, yon lass is a right brick. I'd never 'ave thought she had it in her to work like yon," he said to Annie. Certainly Mama's friends in Priors Ings would have been surprised if they had seen her, garbed and booted and intent upon her task.

As yet, the war was a distant happening in spite of the sombre headlines of the ever-thinning newspapers, and the solemn wireless bulletins. Some food was rationed and the blackout was inconvenient but people's lives went on with a semblance of normality. When changes came they were often changes of omission. The tramps no longer came to live under the viaduct of the bridge for the pea-picking season and the potato harvest. No gypsies knocked on doors to sell

pegs, ribbons and cotton reels. Yet the children in the school playground still sang as they performed their games:

"My mother said that I never should
Play with the gypsies in the wood."

The travelling salesmen and the newspaper canvassers disappeared
and the bands of itinerant actors came no longer to present their
plays in the Town Institute.

Than and Will and their friends continued with their mischievous
pursuits. Mama cut the lavender as usual and put it on top of the
wardrobes to dry. As the war went on the organdie and lace lavender
bags gave way to more utilitarian ones, made from scraps of material
from old dresses. As she had done each year, she carried the tall
white lilies from the garden into the church to fill the altar vases.

An army camp was built outside Priors Ings and its occupants
filled the streets and pubs on weekdays and the church and chapel
on Sundays. The compulsory Church Parades boosted the takings on
the collection plates. More soldiers were stationed at Cowlswick Hall
and Priors Ings seemed to be awash with khaki.

Long army convoys passed through the little town. Some of the
older inhabitants stood and watched the vehicles, trying to work out
how it was that the front ones travelled at a snail's pace but the ones
at the rear had to pelt along at twenty miles an hour in order to keep
up. It was a mystery that was never solved by many of the sightseers.

Shortly after the outbreak of war the local services were mobilised
and co-ordinated in Priors Ings and the surrounding villages. A group
of Local Defence Volunteers, later to become known as the Home
Guard, was formed. These men were either too young or too old to
go into the Forces or were in reserved occupations such as farming.
They met and trained in an area known as the Park which was really
a large field belonging to a farmer. At first the recruits dressed in
civilian clothing and wore armbands bearing the letters LDV. Until
guns were forthcoming they used a variety of sticks and broom-
handles for their drill and manoeuvres.

One Sunday morning the Priors Ings platoon had assembled ready for inspection. Suddenly some of the men flung down their sticks and started to run. Quickly others followed their example in spite of the shouts and commands of their officer. The sergeant when questioned as he ran after the others replied, "There's a wild hoss on the loose an' its coming right at us. If tha' knows what's good for thee, tha'll run as well." With that the officer joined in the flight and they all managed to scramble over a stile before the furious animal reached them.

Local members of the Fire Service were on standby twenty four hours a day and worked on a rota basis. Men who did night duty had to go to work the next morning. This led to many an error and not a few cross words. One tired driver managed to overturn the fire engine into a dyke as he was on the way to a fire. Another fireman, who was running with a hose during an exercise, was told by an officer to get a move on. He replied, "Nah, then! I've milked thirty cows an' fed the hosses afore you got up. I'll have to do the same agen tonight. If tha' puts me on a charge, tha'll have to go an' do my job, if tha' can."

The Air Raid Wardens used to patrol the streets of Priors Ings each night. They made sure that not a chink of light was showing. Like the firemen they had to turn out when the warning sounded at any time of night or day. The Vicar belonged to this group of men and once or twice when the siren sounded on a Sunday, he left his flock to do his duty elsewhere. The Vicar's Warden, who relished the prospect of an Air Raid Warning during Matins or Evensong, took over the lectern with alacrity.

The Police War Reserves or Special Constables were made up of men who, on the whole, were in reserved occupations or too old for the forces. They made a valuable addition to the local constabulary but some got carried away with their newly acquired power. One or two were inclined to dish out summonses for trivial offences and it was said that a few were looking to settle old scores.

One local farmer had a barn in a paddock next door to the Police Station. Here the Sergeant kept his pigeons which thrived on the left-overs after the corn had been threshed. One day at muck-spreading time a farm worker was stopped by a Special Constable and issued with a summons, for dropping muck on the road. He gazed at the Reservist with amazement.

"Nay, that'll never do. Yer might as well tek it back," he said.

"What do you mean?" demanded the constable. "I'm summonsing you for dropping mud on t'road from yer cart."

"Well, nowt'll come of it. Don't yer know that the Sergeant keeps his pigeons in our barn? He won't be right chuffed with thee if he has to shift 'em, will he?" Strange to say, nowt did come of it.

On many of the farms Land Army girls began to take the places of men who had gone into the Forces. As rationing became tighter and more things were in short supply, extra coupons were allowed to the farmers' wives to enable them to give 'drinkings' to the workers at mid-morning and in the afternoon. These usually consisted of mugs of tea and slices of bread and cheese. In some cases the tea was made in a clean bucket. Extra tea, sugar, margarine and bread rations were allowed. Most farmers had their own pigs but they needed a licence to kill one and had to surrender their coupons in lieu of bacon rations.

Many local lads volunteered or were called up for service in the Forces. Aunt Harriet's son Montague, known as Monty, joined the Royal Navy. He was following in a family tradition as his grandfather, Aunt Harriet's father, had been a sea captain. Mama knitted him a long thick scarf in soft navy blue wool, it being unrationed at the time. When Monty came home from his training ship, he shame-facedly admitted that the scarf had been stolen.

"I reported it to an officer," he said, "but he told me that he couldn't do anything about it unless I showed him a photo of the fellow who stole it. I'm sorry, Auntie, because I know what a lot of time and work you put into it."

Mama was shocked at the thought of such dishonesty amongst the members of His Majesty's Royal Navy. She knitted another scarf and this time he guarded it very carefully.

After his training was finished Monty went to sea and served aboard several warships. He was involved in the chase of the *Graf*

Spee, the sinking of the *Bismarck* and he went on harrowing convoys to Russia. When the war ended, he returned unscathed to Priors Ings, much to Aunt Harriet's relief.

Some local lads took longer than others to settle into the routine and discipline of Service life. One innocent was quickly put on a charge as he cycled to his hut from the canteen. He was eating a piece of apple pie, the remainder of his meal, as he bowled along. When he met an officer, he gulped down a mouthful of food and greeted him with a friendly, "How do?" The lad nearly fell off his bicycle in the ensuing furore.

Later in the war, Lantie met a young man who was courting a friend. He was in civilian clothes so she wondered aloud if he was in a reserved occupation or on leave.

"Oh, I'm not in the Forces," he said. "I expect I ought to be, but when my calling-up papers came I was away. My mother opened them and sent them back with a letter saying that I couldn't come because I was on holiday. I never heard from them again. I went and got a job in a munitions factory and the Authorities didn't bother me so I didn't bother them."

The family at the Prior's House listened to the wireless at nine o'clock every evening. The news from France became more ominous as spring gave way to summer. The battles on the Continent and the evacuation of the troops from Dunkirk were described vividly and impressively. There were no television pictures to flash the events into the nation's living rooms. Two or three weeks later all the happenings could be seen on the newsreels at the cinemas in the nearest town. One immediate effect of Dunkirk on Priors Ings and everywhere in the country, was that the church bells were silenced. They would not ring again during the war except to signal an invasion, and an invasion by the Germans was what most people expected.

Yet there were no landings or rumours of landings throughout July and August. Then September came and whilst the harvest was being gathered in, all ears were tuned to the wireless to hear about the Battle of Britain. People listened in homes and shops, in workshops and even in the fields if someone happened to have a portable battery set. The war in the air was too far south to make much impact on those who lived in Priors Ings. All marvelled at the numbers of German planes shot down each day while they enjoyed the long hot summer. There were no dog-fights to be watched in the skies but so descriptive were the accounts broadcast by the war correspondents that everyone felt involved.

As the war hotted up, the railway station at Priors Ings, from whence Lantie, Than and other children travelled to school, became a hive of activity. A great deal of ammunition came in the rail trucks and was sent out in lorries to airfields and army camps all over the county. It was a vital link for the farms and enabled them to send and receive their produce. Day-old chicks came in their thousands. Cattle arrived in trucks and were dispersed to their respective farms. Feeding stuff for the animals arrived with clockwork precision. Potatoes, specially sprayed with a blue dye to show that they were not for human consumption, were unloaded and used to supplement the rations for the cattle.

The corn crops and the pea and potato harvests were loaded into rail trucks and sent to many destinations. Often the farmers had to wait for the next delivery of sacks before they could thresh the corn and bag it. The cereal crops were important for the flour mills and the breweries. Beer was nearly as vital as bread in the war effort. The station at Priors Ings had never been so busy in its entire existence.

One Saturday during the summer of 1940 Mama decided that she and Lantie would go by train to do some shopping in Leeds. Although nothing was said when they left the Prior's House, Lantie knew that they would go to a matinée at one of the theatres. This had been a regular treat for them before the war. After the outbreak of hostilities it was feared that the cities would be heavily bombed and many theatres had closed and the shoppers from the country areas stayed at home. Within a few weeks things seem to be back to normal; the theatres reopened and the shops were ready to welcome customers once again.

Mama did not mention the word 'theatre' to Poppa and Uncle
Tobias before they set out for the station. "They will only worry in
case there is an air raid. We will tell them when we get home."
Mama loved the theatre but seldom went to the cinema. Poppa was
not impressed by the 'Talkies', as he termed them and seldom went
to the theatre. Since his marriage he had been fully occupied with
building up his small business, but he was quite happy for Mama
and Lantie to go out and enjoy themselves.

On this occasion they shopped in the morning, had lunch and
attended a matinée in the afternoon. The play was a comedy-thriller
and they both enjoyed it. Mama loved all kinds of theatre; musicals,
ballet, opera and plays were all grist to her mill. As they walked to
the station she reminisced about seeing *'Chou Chin Chow'* and
'Flora Dora' and other great performances of bygone years.

At the station they met a woman from Priors Ings, a close friend
of Mama's who had been shopping in the city. They all got into a
carriage and settled down, spreading their purchases and bags along
the seats. Lettice, Mama's friend, was very pretty, very lady-like and
of a highly strung nature. She surprised them by diving in amongst
her parcels and producing a large scrubbing brush.

"I had a letter from Charles this morning," she began. The boy
in question was her only son, a pleasant, well-mannered lad and the
apple of his mother's eye. "I think I told you that he had joined the
army and he hopes to get a commission in due course. He is doing
his initial training, he calls it 'square bashing.' Unfortunately he has
encountered some difficulties."

Mama tut-tutted sympathetically.

"Charles wrote to say that he had been in the glasshouse for a
few days. I thought it meant that he had been put on horticultural
duties, but his father says it is army slang for prison. Think of it!
The disgrace! And it is all over nothing of any consequence."

"What happened?" asked Mama, agog to hear the tale.

"It appears that a sergeant had ordered him to scrub a floor.
Charles told him that he could not comply because the scrubbing
brush which was supplied had only twenty-five per cent of its

bristles. The sergeant said that it had fifty per cent of its bristles. Charles disagreed and, as a result, he was taken before an officer and punished. Isn't that awful? I know they have to have discipline, but if Charles said that the brush had only twenty-five per cent of its bristles, then I am sure it was true."

Mama and Lantie made encouraging noises and the story continued:

"I decided that I would go out at once and buy a scrubbing brush with one hundred per cent of its bristles intact. Look what a good strong brush this is," she held it up for them to inspect.

"Tomorrow I shall pack it up with the weekly parcel I send to Charles. Then the next time he is asked to scrub a floor he can use his own brush."

She waved the article aloft once more and put it back into a bag. Then she and Mama began to talk of other matters and Lantie's attention wandered to the passing countryside. It was daylight as they travelled home and she noticed that the names of the stations had been removed. Quite early in the war all the signposts by the roadside had been taken down lest they gave assistance to invaders. Priors Ings needed no signs or name plates and the travellers arrived home in a happy frame of mind after their day out.

When the enemy bombers crossed the east coast the Air Raid Wardens were alerted and the clog mill buzzer wailed its mournful note, even though the planes were miles from Priors Ings. Each night Mama checked that every one had warm clothing and coats beside their beds in case they had to go to the shelter. She kept a special linen bag on a chair beside her bed. Inside it were her marriage lines, the family birth certificates, bank books and Identity Cards. After the first two or three air raid warnings when everyone got up and huddled under the stairs, the querulous notes of the buzzer went unheeded. When a lone plane droned overhead, many people, like Poppa, turned over and muttered, "It's one of ours."

Not for Priors Ings were the nightly bombing raids, the cold shelters or the mass exodus to strange places. For a while the country folks enjoyed a quiet war with few shocks or violent upheavals.

A Quiet War

Occasionally someone would say, "You'd hardly know there was a war on at times, would you now? It's so quiet and peaceful."

Then one day, without any warning, the Wellington bombers roared into the newly completed airfield a mile or so away from Priors Ings and the quiet war was over.

CHAPTER 6

Under the Flight Path

Night after night the heavily laden bombers took off from the nearby aerodrome and flew over the roof tops of Priors Ings. The noise was horrendous and it seemed as if the planes would never become airborne but would hit the chimney pots and crash on the little town. Yet they did rise up and went on to cross the East Coast and head away over the North Sea towards Germany.

Poppa was philosophical about the noise and managed to sleep through the take-offs and returns. "Never mind the din. Remember these young fellows are going out there to help to win the war for us."

Mama agreed but it did not stop her developing insomnia. There were some in Priors Ings who tried to count the bombers as they went out and again when they returned at dawn. The noise continued

60

throughout the war years for the Wellingtons were replaced by Halifaxes and big Liberators flew from another aerodrome a few miles away.

All the activity overhead inspired two young sons of a local farmer and their friend to take precautionary measure with their father's pigs. They reasoned that, as everything on the ground was camouflaged in green and brown, the broad pink backs of the pigs would make a good target for any German bomber that chanced to fly over Priors Ings.

The boys conferred amongst themselves and then spent a busy hour or two painting the pigs green and brown. Their friend had once worked for a local butcher and he was able to use his expertise to hold the animals while the others applied the paint.

Their efforts were not well received. In spite of many protests, "But think of all that pink, it could be seen from an aeroplane a mile off!" they were obliged to remove as much of the paint as possible. The latter task took far longer than the original decoration, in spite of the vigorous use of scrubbing brushes and elbow grease.

Some of the air crews from the aerodrome were billeted in Priors Ings, Tollington and surrounding villages. As with the evacuees, anyone who had a spare room was obliged to take in personnel of one description or another. Will's family had a pilot and his wife staying with them. At dusk the young woman would stand at the sitting room window and watch the bombers as they climbed above the houses. In the mornings she seemed to know that her husband had returned safely.

When they were off-duty, the young people enjoyed themselves. There were balls at the Officers Mess which were occasions of splendour. Such dresses and jewellery had never been seen before in Priors Ings.

On the other hand, some families had much to contend with and found themselves harbouring guests with manners that were quite unacceptable. Will's sister and her family had an officer billeted on them whose behaviour left a lot to be desired. He was very bumptious and tried to organize the home as if it was part of his command.

He boasted that he took a cold bath every morning. One day, Will's sister decided to find out the truth of the matter. She went outside and tested the water with her finger as it gushed down the drain. It was far from cold; lukewarm would have been a charitable description of it.

The officer's wife, who visited him one weekend, behaved in a similarly arrogant manner. She brought bottles of potions and lotions which left stains on a valuable dressing table. No admissions of guilt or regret were forthcoming. Her husband added fuel to the fire by suggesting that the master of the household could not carve a joint properly. He was fortunate that the long suffering landlady did not empty a dish of Yorkshire puddings over his head. But when he came home at night, smelling of drink and unsteady on his feet, his days were numbered in that tolerant but teetotal household. Yet most of those billeted in the little town were friendly, well behaved and appreciative of the hospitality offered to them.

The aerodrome was close to a quiet country road and many Priors Ingites used to take their Sunday afternoon walks in that direction. The security was negligible and folks would stand at gaps in the hedges looking through to see what was going on. Often they had grandstand views of the bombers being loaded up for an evening mission. Some of the names of the bombers were remembered down the decades: 'F for Freddie', 'Dinty Moore', 'Bombers Moon' and many others.

Anyone who stayed at the Prior's House was walked along to see the aerodrome and the bombers. In spite of rationing and wartime shortages, Mama had numerous visitors to stay. Some of her relatives lived in the Potteries and before the war they exchanged frequent visits. Uncle Tobias loved Staffordshire and used to urge Lantie to read the works of Arnold Bennet. "You must read his books if nowt else. They'll tell you all about the Potteries and the Five Towns. A grand read there," he would say.

When war broke out it was deemed safer for the Staffordshire relations to visit Priors Ings than for the family to travel to the Midlands. Aunt Anne, a widow, used to come with her young son

Seth, who was Than's age. He was a well-built lad, fresh faced, tousle-haired and of a friendly disposition. When he was a small boy his mother had bathed him each day in cold water in the deep stone sink in their wash-house. This was in order to toughen his body and purify his soul. As a result he was more sturdy than Than, but the latter could hold his own in their scuffles and horseplay.

Although they got on well together, each time the boys met Than would say through clenched teeth, "Where's my yacht?" This query dated back to a visit made before the war by the Prior's House family to Staffordshire. Than had taken with him his most prized possession, a beautiful model yacht with polished wooden hull and white sails. The boys spent most of their time sailing the boat on a lake in the local park.

At the end of the holiday Mama, who had stayed on with the children for an extra week after Poppa and Uncle Tobias returned home, decided she had too much luggage. The yacht, she ruled, must be left behind. To stop Than's tantrums she said that Seth would bring it the next time he came to Priors Ings. Needless to say the boat never materialised but it was several years before Than's enquiries as to the whereabouts of his treasure ceased.

One Sunday afternoon in the early years of the war, when Seth and his mother were visiting Priors Ings, Mama, Aunt Anne, Seth and Lantie walked through the lanes to the aerodrome. They stood at a gap in the hedge and watched a bomber close by being prepared for the evening take-off. One of the crew came out of the plane and saw Seth. "Want to have look inside, son?" he asked. Seth did not need a second invitation; he scrambled through the hedge and was up into the plane in a flash. Lantie made to follow him but was held back by Mama and Aunt Anne. They were both shocked at the idea of her following after Seth. Young ladies didn't behave like hobble-dehoys.

"Why am I a young lady now and yet last week you said I couldn't go to the dance at the Town Institute because I was a child?" she fumed.

"Because I say so," retorted Mama and turned to speak to Aunt Anne.

Seth came back from his inspection of the Wellington, cock-a-hoop. He was impatient to get home to tell Than what he had missed. That night, as he listened to the bombers taking off, he said, "My Wellington is among that lot. I hope it comes home safely."

Yet it was not one of the young air crew from the aerodrome who caused the biggest sensation of the war in Priors Ings. A couple of miles in the opposite direction from the bomber station was Cowlswick Park, a lightly wooded area covering several acres. One sunny afternoon, a plane circled over the village of Cowlswick. It flew lower and lower until it dipped behind the trees and was lost to sight. Firemen, Home Guards and soldiers from Cowlswick Hall rushed to the place where the aircraft had landed. They noted, with relief, that it was 'one of ours'.

Unconcerned by the commotion around him, a Cowlswick youth clambered out of the cockpit. He grinned at the officer who came forward to interrogate him. After a session of questions and answers he was heard to say cheerily to a group of soldiers, "Keep an eye on it will you? I'm off home to have a cup of tea with my mam."

People in Priors Ings and Cowlswick talked about the incident for months afterwards. It went down in local folklore and was referred to in later years, along with other memories such as 'Them Evacuees', 'The Day the Train was Gunned', as 'When that young fella pinched a plane and landed it in Cowlswick Park'. Everyone had something to say about the matter and ideas differed.

"Fancy pinching a plane! I shouldn't wonder if he could be had up for that."

"Well, he didn't exactly pinch it. He borrowed it, see. He took it back again."

At the time Mama was visiting one of her close friends who was the wife of the local police sergeant. They were chatting over cups of tea when a telephone call came through to the Police Station about the happening in Cowlswick Park. As the telephone was in the hall of the Police House, both ladies sipped their tea and stretched their ears to discover what was afoot. The sergeant kindly enlightened them.

It transpired that when the young plane-taker had come home on his last leave, his friends would not believe that he could fly because he had no wings displayed on his uniform. In vain he pointed out that the white flash in his cap meant that he was a trainee pilot. "Gerron! Tha's kidding", "Pull t'other leg, its got bells on" were some of the kinder remarks.

Stung by their disbelief the young fellow borrowed a plane and landed it in the park just to show everyone that he could fly one.

Mama and her friend sat quietly while the police sergeant got in touch with the boy's station commander. When the latter had recovered from his apoplexy he sent orders that the lad must return the plane at once.

"And he said that it would be woe betide him if he doesn't get it back in the same condition that it left," quoted the sergeant to the two ladies.

That evening, in the gathering dusk, with trees and bushes forming plentiful obstacles, the local hero made a perfect take-off from Cowlswick Park. After circling the village in salute, he headed back to his base.

There was an interval before anyone heard the next instalment of the saga. Plenty of time for rumours to grow and multiply. Perhaps he had been locked up, the local term for being sent to prison. Maybe he had been sent abroad in some menial capacity. After some weeks had passed, the young fellow came on leave and this time he was wearing his pilot's wings. No one could blame him for saying to his erstwhile mockers, "I told you I could fly, didn't I?"

Many attempts were made to bomb the aerodrome and craters appeared from time to time on the runways and in nearby fields. These were filled in very quickly. Early one morning, a lone German plane was seemingly lost on its way back from a raid on a northern city, when the pilot decided to attack Priors Ings.

At half past seven a passenger train standing in the station was machine gunned. Then the plane dropped its last bombs, fortunately incendiaries, in fields between the Prior's House and the river. Fire Fighters and Air Raid Wardens dashed from their homes and places of work.

Some people said that the Clog Mill buzzer had sounded and others swore that it never did. Rumour said that all the windows in the train were smashed. In fact the machine gun fire missed its target and no one was hurt.

Mama was getting breakfast and Than and Lantie were preparing for school when they heard the plane low overhead and the rattle of machine gun fire. Seizing Than, Mama pushed him under the stairs and called for Lantie to join them. In the normal course of events she would have been terrified. As it was she was in search of clean clothes.

"It's no use, I can't come until I've found some clean white socks and a vest," she replied in answer to Mama's entreaties. "Where are my clean clothes? They should be in the drawer. I must have them today because its PT. You know how I hate it. Will you write an excuse note for me, Mama? Oh, do shut up Than. I'm not coming now because it's all over, whatever the noise was. I expect it was one of ours. It's only babies like you who go under the stairs."

She pulled a face at Than who aimed a swipe at her and missed.

Further bickering was prevented by Mama who, though shaken, threatened them both with a box on the ears if they didn't hurry up and have breakfast and get off to school.

Every evening that week and at the weekend, scores of people from Priors Ings walked up to the river and stood looking from the bridge to see where the bombs had dropped. It was pleasant to speculate after the event what might have happened if the bombs had been of the high explosive kind. Would all or only half of Priors Ings have been blown up? Certainly the Prior's House and Annie's cottage would have gone for they were the two buildings nearest to the river. The old church would have been badly damaged and who knows how many houses would have been blown up. And was the train hit or not? If it wasn't hit, where did the bullets go? If it was hit, where were the holes? Priors Ings talked about The Day the Bombs Dropped for many months after the event.

Under the Flight Path

Later in the war, far more serious happenings occurred and everyone learned how dangerous life could be under the flight path. One night an aircraft carrying a full load of bombs crashed before it could get airborne, near the village of Tollington. Some of the crew came from overseas and were buried in the local churchyard. An ammunition dump exploded on another occasion and the noise was heard for miles around. Many personnel were killed and shocked villagers realised that the war had come to their bit of England.

And every morning after they had been out on their bombing raids the surviving planes came home to their base. Some returned intact; others limped home with parts of their fuselages or tails shot away and with the dead or dying still inside. Many never came back. Yet, within hours the planes were repaired or replaced and other young men arrived to take the places of those who would fly no more. Down the years of the war, the relentless drone of planes sounded over Priors Ings and all the surrounding villages. Nobody grumbled any more about the noise and everyone was only too thankful that the planes were 'ours' and not 'theirs'.

CHAPTER 7

Soldiering On

"Spam! Snoek! Ugh! The very names are enough to put anyone off. Have you any corned beef, my love?"

Poppa took sandwiches and a flask of tea to work and, as food rationing began to make people tighten their belts, Mama's ingenuity was sorely taxed to vary the family diet.

A vegetable plot in a clearing in the orchard provided a variety of greens, root crops and the ubiquitous potato. With these Mama was able to make the meat ration go a long way. Potatoes and carrots were promoted by the Ministry of Food as the Staff of Life. Woolton Pie, named after the Minister of the Department, made a filling meal but it was not one of the family's favourites. It consisted of a casserole of vegetables topped with a crust of mashed potatoes.

The hens provided eggs which, together with her store of hoarded sugar, enabled Mama to make cakes and sponges. Nobody was allowed to have sugar in their tea, coffee or cocoa. Sometimes when one of the hens had reached the end of its egg-laying life, it was killed and provided a welcome addition to the diet.

Although the family ration books were registered for groceries with Uncle Joshua, Mama never asked for any extra food and Aunt Margaret did not offer any. "Every ounce has to be accounted for to the Ministry. Every ounce!" the latter would state dramatically from time to time. She made no mention of the large families in the district who were unable to afford even the small amounts of butter and sugar they were allowed.

Even in Priors Ings there was a small but active Black Market in food and clothing coupons, but such transactions did not extend outside the town to the Prior's House. Mama made do with an exchange of goods between herself and the ladies of her acquaintance. The orchard provided plenty of fruit and people were happy to swap some sugar or dried fruit for a few eggs, Bramley apples or Victoria plums.

One winter's evening Poppa returned home from work, had his evening meal and settled into his armchair with his pipe.

"Wouldn't it be fine to have a nice big ham in the pantry once again?" he said to Mama.

"Not much chance of that until the war is over," she replied, busily turning the heel of a sock she was knitting.

"Well, I don't know, we might be able to manage something in that line. I think I could arrange an exchange. Can you save up two dozen eggs and sort out a stone of Bramleys, half a stone of eating apples and the same of pears from the loft? If we can have them ready by the end of next week I might be able to swap them for a ham. Someone at work is killing a pig."

Whether this animal was killed legally or illegally was not mentioned. Strict licensing governed the killing of pigs but country people knew that the inspectors could not be everywhere and count every pig in the district.

Mama was eager and interested but terrified. "What if someone

69

finds out? You could go to prison! Oh! I would rather starve than have that happen. No, no, we mustn't do such a thing."

Poppa, calm as ever, reassured her. "No money is changing hands. It is barter; perhaps not legal but not exactly illegal. And you children, not a word to anyone, mark you."

Poppa had no need to caution Uncle Tobias who knew when to hold his peace. Lantie and Than, like Mama, were far too afraid of the consequences of being found out to betray the secret.

Several days later a stranger came to the back door after dark. He came on a bicycle with a large basket on the front and another on the carrier at the back. He and Poppa carried parcels through the dark conservatory and the dimly lit hall into the pantry. From a room leading off the conservatory they conveyed other parcels out across the garden to the back gate. Then the stranger mounted his bicycle and disappeared into the night.

The family gathered round the stone slab in the pantry and watched Poppa open the parcels. As well as a ham there were a couple of small packages containing sausages and chitterlings. What bounty lay before their eyes and what hopes of feasts for the future!

Alas, for the clandestine dealings; it turned out that the ham had been hastily cured and it went bad. When Poppa related this news to the purveyor of the goods, he was told to bury it in the garden or orchard and dig it up after three months when it would be found to have been miraculously cured.

"It's an old custom what country folks has used for years," declared the pig owner. Poppa did bury the ham in the orchard but he never dug it up again as nobody fancied eating it no matter how meagre the meat rations became.

"It's a punishment from the Almighty for dealing in Black Market goods," declared Mama, but Uncle Tobias told her not to be so daft.

When the war had been on for several months parcels began to arrive from America. They came at irregular intervals and were received with great excitement. After the Great War Poppa had spent some years working in the States. He had had an interesting job as chauffeur to a millionaire and he was very happy with his life there.

His employer wanted him to stay in America and he offered to pay Mama's fare to go there and also promised to provide them with a house. Because she was the only surviving daughter of grandma's Victorian family, Mama was duty bound to look after her mother and was unable to leave her. As a result Poppa gave up his job and returned to England. They were married and he settled in Priors Ings and set up his own small garage and engineering business.

Every Christmas his old employer wrote to the family wishing them well and offering Poppa a job if ever he changed his mind and wanted to return to America. It was from this kind and generous man that the wartime parcels came.

There was much excitement at the Prior's House when the first parcel arrived. Among other items it contained a tin of butter. "That will do to make a Christmas cake," said Mama, happily.

There was a large tin of salmon, one of ham and another of tinned chunks of beef. There were biscuits, sweets, sugar, coffee and tea. The tea caused Mama some perplexity as it was contained in numerous small bags. Sitting at the kitchen table she cut open each little tea bag and carefully deposited the contents into the tea caddy.

"What a silly way to pack tea," she exclaimed from time to time.

As the war continued, life in Priors Ings revolved round the routine of blackouts, rationing and generally making do. At the Prior's House Lantie and Than played and quarrelled and travelled to school on the train, enjoying life in the unthinking way of the young as the momentous events of the conflict came and went.

The wireless was a great source of news and solace, for the newspapers seemed to be out-of-date before they arrived. The speeches of Winston Churchill and the talks by J. B. Priestley, so solid and reassuring after the Sunday evening news, were listened to avidly.

Comedy programmes such as 'ITMA' and 'Bandwagon' helped to lighten the general gloom. If Mama became pessimistic, as she was wont to do from time to time, Poppa would tease her gently by saying, "Ah! it's being so cheerful that keeps us going," which was one of his favourite quotations from 'ITMA'. When he prepared to shave Uncle Tobias each evening, for the latter never went to the barber's shop, Poppa would try to cheer him up with another, saying "Can I do you now, Sir?" but it had little effect for Uncle Tobias disliked the shaving routine at the best of times.

Mama, on the other hand, loved to listen to the romantic songs sung by Anne Zeigler and Webster Booth and they all enjoyed musical items by John McCormack and Richard Tauber.

Sometimes Poppa twiddled the knobs on the wireless and the voice of William Joyce, nicknamed Lord Haw Haw, came over loud and clear. The children liked to imitate his nasal tones "Jairmany calling, Jairmany calling", but everyone tired very quickly of listening to his tirades.

As well as the aerodrome at Tollington, there was an army camp nearby and many soldiers were stationed at Cowlswick Hall. Every evening Priors Ings was full of soldiers and airmen who filled the pubs and wandered through the darkened streets. Yet the women of the little town felt no fear as they went about the familiar byways. Mama went regularly to the Town Institute to do Canteen Duty with the other ladies. She came home through the blacked out streets using a dimmed flashlight. Sometimes Poppa met her at the top of the lane leading to the Prior's House and escorted her home. Perhaps country bred people, being used to the dark and knowing everyone in the town, had no built-in fears of their fellow men in those wartime days.

The only illumination came from the searchlights which swept the skies when there was an Air Raid Warning. These lights made folks feel uneasy because they reckoned they sent a signal to German planes that something of importance lay below.

"They'll attract them planes like moths to a candle," was the general verdict.

Posters were displayed everywhere, on hoardings, in the Town Institute and the station waiting rooms, warning about the dangers that lurked, even in Priors Ings.

"Careless talk costs lives. Be like Dad, keep Mum."

"Is your journey really necessary?"

"Dig for Victory."

There were posters for National Savings Weeks when the populace was urged to invest its money during Warships Week, War Weapons Week, Wings for Victory Week and many such special savings drives. Everyone was urged to "Lend not Spend".

One afternoon a week an official National Savings Collector called at the Prior's House selling National Savings Stamps. After they had had a cup of tea and a chat, Mama would buy two half crown stamps from the lady. These were stuck on cards, one for Than and one for Lantie. When each card carried fifteen shillings worth of stamps it was exchanged at the Post Office for a National Savings Certificate. Not only did these transactions help the war effort but they built up a little nest egg for the children at the same time. After the war, when they were older, Mama gave them the certificates which they cashed to finance trips abroad.

Volunteers were needed to take part in the Red Cross Penny-a-Week collection scheme. Mama was asked to cover certain streets in Priors Ings. She decided that this was a task that Lantie could do. Protests about having too much homework were dismissed out of hand. Mama pointed out that the whole area could be worked in half an hour and she could do the round on Friday evenings. Homework for that night could be done on Saturday mornings.

"It's not fair! It will mess up my whole weekend," grumbled Lantie.

"Stop saying 'It's not fair!" snapped Mama who was worn out battling with a recalcitrant teenager. "When you grow up you will discover that life is never fair and your lot in life is far better than that of many others."

Lantie set off with her Red Cross tin and ambled round the back of the churchyard. She wandered up Mill Street and Butter Market and into Market Place. She knocked on doors in High Street and Church Lane and went through a snicket to Priory Lane and Old Hall Farm. At first it took her less than half an hour and the penny-a-week was adhered to literally by the donors. Gradually the amount was increased to twopence or threepence and one affluent household contributed sixpence.

Lantie found that she enjoyed doing the Red Cross round and talking to people on their doorsteps. Some of the older folk asked her to step indoors. "Just coom in for a minute or two, lass. It makes a change to have a bit of a chat."

She would emerge twenty minutes later and hurry on to the next house. The half hour task lengthened into an hour and then to two hours as the calls grew longer. Sometimes Mama would grow anxious and send Than to look for her. He knew the regular stopping places and winkled her out in a short time with the laconic message "Supper's ready".

When clothing coupons were introduced they were spent more frugally than money. Poppa and Uncle Tobias made do with the clothes they had but occasionally they needed coupons for shoes. The children were still growing and most of the family coupons went on their needs. Some materials were coupon-free including an oily off-white wool which was said to be used to make stockings for seamen. This was soaked and washed to remove the oil and then it was knitted up into sweaters and cardigans.

Parachute silk was sometimes available and, for anyone with patience to unpick the panels, the material could be made into underwear. The colours were not very attractive, ranging from green to off-white but a coupon-free bargain was not to be scorned.

The colour khaki seemed to predominate in the streets of Priors Ings and a few of the uniformed men found their way to the Prior's House to partake of wartime hospitality. Perhaps it was Mama's sweet friendly face and sympathetic ear that led the young soldiers at the Institute canteen to confide in her. Some were homesick and anxious to find accommodation so that their parents could visit them for a few days. Mama and the ladies consulted together and were able to recommend respectable lodgings when the hostelries were full. On more than one occasion she made room for the parents of young soldiers at the Prior's House. She would never take payment for these guests because she regarded it as part of her war work.

Soldiering On

She was fond of saying, "After all, it might have been Than wanting us to visit him if he had been older."

Invitations to visit the Prior's House for tea and supper were offered and accepted. Poppa worked with military personnel and at the weekends he would bring home a young soldier for tea and a pleasant evening by the fireside. Thus, friendships were formed between erstwhile strangers.

Some of the young men who came to the Prior's House were musically inclined and they enjoyed playing the piano. Many a pleasant hour was spent with the family and friends and a uniformed figure coaxing tunes from the old fashioned instrument.

Mama loved these gatherings and the interest and stimulation of conversation that strangers brought to the everyday routine. Although rationing caused her many a headache it did not diminish the warmth of her welcome. "Just think, it might have been Than," she declared yet again when another soldier or airman joined the family circle.

As it happened it was Than who brought one of the most interesting characters to the Prior's House. When he was fourteen years old Than developed a belated interest in music. A couple of years of lessons and much chivvying from Mama had turned him into a mediocre piano player. Suddenly he expressed a desire to learn to play the organ. Lessons were arranged with the church organist and Than became a very keen pupil.

The organ at Priors Ings church was really half a very large organ. Its sounds could fill the huge building with deafening notes. One Saturday afternoon Than went into the church to practise and found that someone was playing the organ. Quietly he walked past the choir stalls and across the chancel. He saw a soldier seated at the raised bench, a man much older than the young fellows he encountered in the streets.

Than listened and watched until the organist sensed his presence and stopped playing.

"I've got permission to play the organ but you can take over if you wish," said the man answering the boy's unspoken question.

"No, play something else; play some more Handel, full blast," replied Than.

The soldier played many requests from Than and then he rose from the seat and motioned to him to take his place. The boy declined, lacking confidence to follow such an exhibition of talent. He watched silently as the organ was closed and locked.

"I'll drop the key in at the Vicarage on my way past. I expect you have one of your own," remarked the soldier.

"Where are you billeted?" asked Than.

"At Cowlswick Hall. Did you know it was haunted? Some of my chaps swear they have seen ghosts, and who am I to contradict them? I'm joining the choir tomorrow," he added as an afterthought.

"Come round to our house for tea this afternoon," urged Than, eager to show off his new acquaintance to the family. "It's all right, we often have folks for tea and supper, soldiers and airmen and lots of visitors. My parents like company."

"Now, laddie, you mustn't go around asking strange soldiers to tea," said the man.

"Oh, come on," pleaded Than. "Mama won't mind and you can play our piano."

The soldier smiled at the boy's friendliness, but he said, "You go home and ask your Mother if you may invite me to tea sometime. I shall be here for Matins tomorrow so you can tell me what she says. Now you had better hop off home or they will wonder where you are. My name's Clark, by the way, Walter Clark. Did you know that all Clarks in the army are nicknamed 'Nobby', just as all Whites are known as 'Chalky'. Names are funny, aren't they?"

Than told him his name and they went outside together and parted at the churchyard gates.

Next morning Than was at church early. He scrambled into his cassock and surplice and then hung around the gates, scrutinising the khaki-clad figures as they filed into the building. At last he saw his new acquaintance coming along Market Place and raced to meet him.

"It's all right. Mama says you can come to tea today. You can stay for supper as well. And I forgot to tell you that I'm in the choir too."

So began a friendship which developed between Walter and Than's family and lasted for decades after the war. That night saw the first of many musical evenings with the soldier taking charge. He had a fine baritone voice, played the piano expertly and was a clever mimic and raconteur. There was always much laughter in the Prior's House when he was present.

Walter made much of Uncle Tobias and persuaded him to join everyone in the sitting room. Normally the old man preferred to stay with his books and papers in the kitchen or the living room.

To Walter's accompaniment they all sang heartily; 'Dolly Gray' and the songs of the Boer War led to tunes from the Great War. They started with Poppa's favourites, 'Pack Up Your Troubles' and 'Keep The Home Fires Burning' and then they went on to the beautiful melodies of Stephen Forster. Walter did not use any music when he played the piano and he managed to satisfy most requests.

They sang the songs of the present conflict but all agreed that 'Run Rabbit Run', 'The White Cliffs of Dover' and 'We'll Meet Again', though tuneful enough, could not beat the songs of yesteryear.

Walter was a Londoner in his late thirties and a bachelor when Than met him. Before the war he had lived at home and cared for his elderly parents. He had been in the Reserves and had been called up at the outbreak of hostilities. He was sent overseas in 1939 and came back from the Middle East to find himself at Cowlswick Hall. He had many strange and amusing tales to tell. He revelled in being the centre of attention and Lantie heard Poppa remark quietly to Mama that he should have been an actor instead of an architect.

Sometimes Walter lapsed into a serious mood, especially when he spoke of his own war experiences. When Lantie asked him what was his favourite piece of music, knowing that his repertoire was very wide, she received an unexpected reply.

"I love many pieces of music, both choral and instrumental, and I could not pick a favourite. But I can tell you the most wonderful sound I ever heard, the most marvellous music of my life so far. It was the sound of the bagpipes of the 51st Highland Division coming to relieve us at the siege of Tobruk."

This seige was the longest in British Military history and lasted for two hundred and forty-two days. The family fell silent for a few minutes as they pondered the matter.

Walter spent Christmas at the Prior's House and a jolly, merry Christmas it was. Shortly afterwards he was posted overseas again. After the war when he was demobbed, he emigrated to Australia where he had a brother who was a vicar. He pursued his career as an architect and developed his musical talents in Operatic Societies and Choirs. He wrote long, interesting letters of his life Down Under and when he came back to England for a holiday, after being away for many years, he came to Priors Ings.

All the family gathered at the Prior's House and for a short time they re-lived the happy memories of his wartime visits.

It was on Sundays that the inhabitants of Priors Ings realised just how many service personnel there were in the district. They came to church and chapel, filling the buildings and boosting the takings on the collection places. Church Parade was compulsory so some attended with less eagerness than others.

The military presence was particularly noticeable in church on Armistice Sunday. November the 11th, Armistice Day, was the day on which the Great War ended in 1918. The eleventh hour of the eleventh day of the eleventh month was known and revered by the whole country. Before the Second War, if the date fell on a weekday, everything came to a halt for two minutes at eleven o'clock. Children stood silent in their playgrounds or classrooms; pedestrians stopped in the streets and drivers of vehicles pulled up at the kerbsides. Everyone remembered with sadness and respect those who had fallen in the Great War. Poppies were worn and scarlet wreaths appeared and even the young ones were overawed in those two minutes of silence.

If Armistice Day fell on a Sunday, the old soldiers of Priors Ings and surrounding hamlets gathered outside the British Legion rooms in Market Place. They lined up and marched in formation, chests ablaze with medals, to Church or Chapel for a Service of Remembrance.

Poppy wreaths were placed below the Rolls of Honour. In Priors Ings Church there were two such Rolls. One was of marble and bore the names of all those who had been killed during the war. Two brothers were from one family and three from another. At the back of the church another board listed all who had left the district to serve their King and Country. The names of those who did not return were marked with a gold star. Poppa's name was on this board for, although he had been born in Surrey, it was from Priors Ings that he had gone to join the army.

At a crucial point in the church service, an old soldier, 'Codge' Clayton, would sound the Last Post and Reveille, as he stood under the tower at the west end of the church. The fact that the notes were wobbly and the cornet gave out cracked sounds only made the occasion more poignant.

All this changed during the Second World War. It was no longer possible for the country to come to a standstill at eleven o'clock on November the 11th. Remembrance of the Fallen in the past and present conflicts was confined to the nearest Sunday to Armistice Day.

On these wartime occasions the huge church was full. Service personnel occupied the nave pews and overflowed into the pews in two side aisles. One year a Brigade of Guards was stationed nearby and arrived at the church headed by their own band. Army trumpeters took the place of Codge's cornet and the whole ceremony was huge and impressive. Yet, in after years, it was the simple British Legion services and Codge playing his cornet under the massive old tower that people remembered with affection.

At the end of the proceedings the National Anthem was played by the Guards band and the whole congregation stood to attention. One Remembrance Sunday, as the family walked home after the service, Mama said thoughtfully, "You know, dear, I don't think these young soldiers stand to attention as smartly as you older ones. Some of them looked a bit sloppy during the National Anthem."

To which Poppa replied, teasingly, "Oh yes, my love, they were standing to attention well enough. It was their uniforms that were standing at ease." Mama cast him a suspicious glance, unsure whether he was teasing her or not. She walked on in silence and they all went back to the Prior's House and the prospect of Sunday lunch.

CHAPTER 8

Growing Up

"It's not fair," grumbled Lantie as she sat at the table and scribbled furiously. Her school satchel was on the floor and her books and papers were scattered around the kitchen.

"Now what's the matter?" demanded Mama. "You're forever grumbling about something or other these days."

"I've got to write some lines and hand them in first thing in the morning. Everyone in the class has to do them. The Geography teacher came into the room and there was an awful noise so she gave lines to the whole class. It's not fair because some of us were quiet. I had my desk lid up and I was looking at a 'Picturegoer' someone had lent me."

"Well, the lines will punish the wrongdoers and be a warning to the others," said Mama. "What have you got to write?"

"Good manners and quiet behaviour are two characteristics of civilized human beings, thirty times," snapped Lantie. "It will be branded on my brain for ever."

Mama sighed and went through to the sitting room, wondering, not for the first time, if other mothers found life with a teenage daughter as difficult as her own. Hardly a week passed without a confrontation with Lantie and as they both had volatile temperaments there were many stormy scenes which ended in tears.

Lantie and Than attended a grammar school about ten miles from Priors Ings. Like other similar establishments in the thirties and forties, it had high standards of discipline and work. The academic excellence was reflected in the long lists of names on the Honours Board. Countless pupils had won County Major Scholarships to Oxford, Cambridge and many of the old universities.

Most of the teachers at the school had one or more degrees and they were all dedicated to their work. The children of that era were doubly fortunate in so far as they were well taught and had the continuity of the same teachers down the years. They had the security of knowing that, at the beginning of each school year, most, if not all, the familiar faces would be present at assembly.

The school was co-educational but up to the outbreak of war the boys and girls were taught separately until they reached the fifth form. Some masters went into the Forces and their places were taken by women or older men. Later the classes were mixed throughout the school but the standards remained as high as ever.

Whilst Lantie's temperament was a trial to Mama, Than was a worry to her in different ways. He had not managed to gain a scholarship for the grammar school but, after much private tutoring and many exhortations from Mama, he passed the entrance examination and was admitted as a paying pupil. Both children needed school uniforms, clothes for Physical Education and many extras which placed a strain on the family finances. As a result pocket money was restricted and it was Than, the young entrepreneur, who looked for ways to supplement his weekly allowance.

At first, on the strength of his music lessons, he applied for and got a job as organist at Cowlswick church. One so young was only considered because of his undoubted ability to play for Matins and Evensong, and the fact that there was no one else for the post. For two weeks Than cycled to and fro to Cowlswick, a matter of two miles away, for Sunday Services and choir practices.

He was delighted to earn some real money. However, Mama decided that the organist's job was coming between Than and his homework and he was obliged to resign.

His next venture into the world of work was a Saturday job with one of the local butchers. Butcher John, as he was known, was a large impressive looking man who ran a flourishing business in Market Place. Unfortunately Than did not have the dedication required to make an ideal butcher's boy.

The meat ration was very small but Than's habit of popping it through the letter boxes if the occupants of the houses were out, resulted in one or two complaints. This was so, in one case, when the dog opened up the parcel and ate the family's meat ration for a week. At one of his regular calls Than had to manoeuvre his way past a fierce dog on the end of a long chain. One day, to pacify the furious animal, he broke off a link from a string of sausages and flung it to the dog as a peace offering. Mindful that he would have to pass it again on his way back, he reserved a second sausage to ensure a safe return. The lady of the house received her order without noticing the discrepancy. She remarked placidly, "Eeh! Yon meat ration gets smaller every week, don't it? We shall soon have nowt but corned beef and spam."

Than's job lasted for a few Saturdays but one morning it ended rather abruptly. Arriving back at the shop to collect another basketful of orders, he went past the large freezer and absent mindedly slammed the door shut. He was unaware that Butcher John was inside the cold store sorting out the meat. It was some minutes before he was missed and there was no handle on the inside of the freezer. By the time someone realised where he was and released him, his shock of hair and large white moustache were frozen so hard that he resembled Santa Claus without his costume.

By a process of elimination Than was identified as the culprit. He agreed he must have closed the door but could not recollect doing it. The butcher decided there and then that he was able to dispense with his services. Mama felt obliged to apologise for Than's shortcomings when next she went to collect the family meat ration. Butcher John did not bear any grudge but he remarked,

"Nay, it's plain to see that the lad's not cut out for butchering."

One lasting effect of the job was that Than could never again bear to eat brawn. "Ugh! You should see how it is made," he said to Lantie. "There was this great big copper in which the sheeps' or pigs' heads were boiled. When it had cooled down you had to put your hand into the mixture and fish out the eyes and bones and goodness knows what else. It was revolting. I'll never eat brawn again as long as I live."

After that foray into commerce Than concentrated on his rabbits and bantams. He won several prizes at the local Fur and Feathers shows. As both he and Lantie had their pocket money supplemented by contributions from Uncle Tobias they managed to finance most of their needs.

One day Than came home from school in high spirits.

"Mama, guess what? I've broken the Long Jump record in the school sports."

"Well done," congratulated Mama, "but remember that long jumping won't get you through your examinations. You must concentrate on your studies as much as you do on sport." Anything that came between Than and his academic work was an anathema to Mama, whether it was athletics, rugby or cricket. Than was very good at all sports and the Long Jump record he set that day was not broken for over twenty years.

Meanwhile Lantie managed to aggravate and defy Mama at every possible opportunity. She would refuse to do any household tasks and only the threat of having her pocket money stopped made her tidy her room and conform to the routine of the household.

Most of her leisure time was spent with her head in a book. She had read all the interesting ones in the Prior's House and borrowed a number from Aunt Margaret's horde of volumes. Every week she went down the Chapel Path to the Council School where her cousin Freda ran the County Library. Even these sources of books were not enough to satisfy her appetite.

Near the station where the children caught a train home to Priors Ings at the end of the school day, was the Silver Library. Here could be borrowed, for the sum of twopence, a book for a week. As Lantie's pocket money was limited she was constrained to choose one or two a week. Gradually she worked her way through numerous Westerns by Zane Grey, the saga of *Anne of Avonlea* and the sequels, detective novels and the romantic fiction of Ethel M. Dell and her contemporaries. Everything was grist to the mill, from Dickens to Mrs. Henry Wood. She spent hours poring over *War and Peace* and provoked another scene at home by wanting to re-christen the cats Natasha and Nicholas.

"Call them what you like, but they will only come when called Tibs and Fluffy," retorted Mama. "In any case, they are both she-cats so it's ridiculous to call one Nicholas. Call them anything you want, I'm just tired of your fads and fancies."

One Friday night Lantie came home with a copy of Margaret Mitchell's *Gone With The Wind*. She was enthralled by it and read late into the night.

All day Saturday she was absorbed by the story of Scarlett and Rhett. On Sunday morning she pleaded a headache to avoid going to church.

"I don't wonder you've a headache after all that reading. Have you done your weekend homework?" demanded Mama.

"I'll do it this afternoon when my headache has gone," replied Lantie. Mama was exasperated but left her in charge of the Sunday lunch.

"Don't touch the joint, it will be all right in the oven. Put the pan of potatoes on the hob at half past eleven and the steamer with the other vegetables on top of the pan at ten to twelve," she instructed.

Uncle Tobias, after busying himself with some matters in the loft, gathered up the Sunday papers and took them through into the sitting room where he settled down to read in peace. Lantie dashed upstairs for her book and sat by the fire, absorbed once more in the tale of the Deep South.

At eleven fifteen, she glanced at the clock and decided that the potatoes might as well go on the fire hob while she remembered them. Then she went back to her book.

Very shortly afterwards, or so it seemed, the kitchen door crashed open and she was aware of a smell of burning. Mama, dressed in her Sunday finery, rushed in, seized the pan of potatoes and ran through the conservatory. She flung the blackened pan and its contents on to the garden.

Mama stormed and raged and, in her temper, would have flung the book on to the fire if she had not known it was from the library.

"You can leave that book down here and go straight to your room. Headache indeed! You can stay up there without any lunch until I decide when you can come down."

After Mama's temper had cooled, more potatoes were peeled to replace the burnt offerings. When lunch was ready Than was sent upstairs to tell Lantie that she could come down and eat if she apologised for her disgraceful behaviour and washed all the dishes after the meal.

"Shan't," she said to him, but she thought better of it. After further recriminations from Mama, peace reigned for the rest of the day.

Several months later, Lantie came home from school looking very thoughtful. After supper she offered to clear the table and wash the dishes. The next day was Saturday and she asked Mama if she needed any shopping doing in Priors Ings and if she should prepare the vegetables for lunch. Again she helped to clear away after the meal and dry the dishes. By this time Mama's suspicions were well aroused.

"Now, what are you up to? What is this all about? You want something, I'll be bound."

"Can I go to the pictures with Nan next Saturday afternoon, please?" asked Lantie humbly. Nan was her best friend at school.

"I don't see why not. You have your train pass and your pocket money. As long as it is a matinee," replied Mama in a reasonable tone of voice.

"Well, you see Mama, we want to go to Doncaster to see 'Gone With The Wind'. I would have to have the bus fare which is one and sixpence return as well as my train pass, and the tickets are three and sixpence each. It is a four hour film and they have put up the prices and – – –"

"Three and sixpence! Three and sixpence to go to the pictures! I've never heard anything like it!" interrupted Mama. "What with the ticket and the bus fare it will be five shillings. No! I'm afraid that is too much!"

"Oh, please Mama, please let me go. It's a very special film. I'll go without my pocket money for a week if you will give me two weeks next week. Oh! and we shall need sandwiches because there is an interval half way through the film," she added as an after-thought.

"We'll see what your Poppa has to say about it. I don't know that he will want you two young girls gadding off all that way to the pictures."

Lantie and her friend went to see the film and were thrilled as they watched the book brought to life by Vivien Leigh, Clark Gable, Leslie Howard and others. They gasped at the spectacular burning of Atlanta and wept at the death of Melanie Wilkes. As they munched their sandwiches during the interval they assured each other that it was worth every penny of the money they had spent. Whether Mama thought the same when she was regaled with an ecstatic account of the film was a matter for doubt.

During her early teens Lantie's relationship with Mama was a mixture of compromise and confrontation. She would coax her to let her use some make-up, albeit only Pond's cream and powder and she would sometimes dab herself with Mama's scent, 4711 or Evening in Paris.

Occasionally she borrowed items of Mama's clothing, especially her silk stockings for special events such as the school Christmas parties. Not that any of these fripperies did much good for her ego.

At home Lantie was secure and confident and had plenty to say in her own environment. She did not realise what a plain Jane she was until it came to social events. Then she was either tongue tied or too garrulous. With her straight hair and nondescript appearance she found herself time and time again among the wallflowers and trying not to care.

"I hate parties, I just hate them," she said tearfully to Mama after yet another miserable evening.

"Never mind, my love, you'll enjoy them when you are older. Growing up is very hard," comforted Mama.

Meanwhile, far away from Priors Ings, the war raged on in the Middle and Far East. News of distant battles came over the wireless and victories and defeats were bolstered by Churchillian rhetoric. The losses of ships at sea became more and more worrying and everyone was urged to tighten their belts.

Morale was kept up by such shows as 'Bandwagon', 'ITMA', 'Music While You Work' and 'Monday Night at Eight'. Even the Brains Trust gave people a feeling of security. The catch phrases from 'Garrison Theatre' with the comedian Jack Warner's, 'Mind My Bike' and 'di-da-di-da' and from the Hippodrome 'Let me tell you' were on everyone's lips.

Minor excitements occurred from time to time. One November day in 1942, the bells of Priors Ings Church, which had not rung out since September 1939, sent forth their peals to signal the victory of Montgomery and the troops at El Alamein.

"Isn't it wonderful to hear the bells again? When will they ring every Sunday as they used to?" people asked each other.

"Not until the war ends, whenever that might be. Yet it is a good job they don't ring, because that would mean that the Germans were invading us. They'll ring one day when peace comes," said Poppa.

Even so, spirits flagged from time to time as one grey year followed another. Lantie heard an old man remark to Uncle Tobias, "It seems like this war will never end. I wonder if thee and me will see it through?"

Yet everyone in Priors Ings realised how lucky they were not to have to endure the heavy bombing to which the nation's cities were subjected. They were comforted by the roar of the bombers which took off nightly from Tollington airfield for raids on the Continent. A "Bomber's Moon" may have brought fear to the people in German cities but to Priors Ings folk it meant that their lads were going out to help to win the war.

One Christmas Poppa had to make the long journey down to his native county of Surrey to attend the funeral of his father. He travelled by train and crossed London in the middle of a heavy air raid. He came home greatly saddened, not only at the loss of his remaining parent but by the sights he had seen in the battered capital.

"The destruction, the dust, the fires and the smells, you would hardly believe it," he told the family. "There were people huddled together on the platforms of the underground stations, hundreds of people. They had their gas masks, blankets, food and drink. They go down there every night as soon as the air raid sirens sound. Some go down there every night whatever happens and lie on the hard stone or on makeshift beds. Poor souls! Their war is so much harder than ours. We have a lot for which to be thankful."

The following summer Mama and Poppa ventured down to Surrey to stay with his favourite sister Frances and her family. In any large family some siblings are closer to one than to the others and so it was with Poppa and his sister.

The children loved to visit Aunt Frances in her delightful white house with the old firemark high up over the front door. Poppa explained to them how, in olden times, people who insured against fire put an iron plate on their house. If there was a fire and the engine crew saw the mark, they would do their duty. If the house had no firemark they would go away and let the fire do its worst.

There was a large lawn in front of the house and the grass stretched on either side of the buildings. A colourful herbaceous border flourished on one side of the drive and flower beds and tubs splashed more colour on either side of the front door and under the windows. At the back, a path led down to a large vegetable bed, soft fruit trees and a small orchard. A stream at the bottom separated the property from the next door garden. Aunt Frances's garden was a beautiful place where weeds were seldom seen and everything was immaculate. This was not really surprising as her husband, Uncle Perce, was head gardener at one of the large country houses in a nearby village. He would not have allowed his own garden to be anything but pristine and perfect.

While Mama and Poppa were staying with Aunt Frances and Uncle Perce, their younger son Roy came home on leave. He was a Sergeant Airgunner, a quiet, artistic young man with a lovely sense of humour.

When he had joined the Air Force there were doubts as to whether he would be accepted for air crew as he had not had a grammar school education. Aunt Frances asked the squire of the village if he would write a testimonial for her son. Armed with this letter Roy left home. He was accepted and began his training for air crew duties. When he sent his civilian clothes home his mother found the letter, unopened, in a pocket of his jacket. He had passed on his own merits. Mama and Poppa came home full of praise for the young man.

"Such a lovely boy," exclaimed Mama. "So quiet and well mannered, yet full of fun."

A week later Lantie came downstairs to find Mama sitting at the kitchen table weeping copiously. She was holding a letter in her hand. Poppa, looking desolate, stood by the fireplace.

Without a word, Mama handed the letter to Lantie. It was a brief note from Aunt Frances to say that Roy was missing, believed killed.

"He was such a fine young man," wept Mama.

"So are they all," said Poppa sadly.

Years later, when Lantie was staying with Aunt Frances, she had an insight into the depth of her sorrow.

"I cried every day for over a year," she said. "I washed with my tears, I ironed with my tears. I scrubbed with my tears and I baked with my tears. And still I cried, though I knew that all the tears in the world would never bring him back."

Growing Up

So many thousands more had wept their oceans of tears as well as dear Aunt Frances. Lantie could begin to understand the sufferings of those who had lost their loved ones, because, by that time, she had long since grown up.

CHAPTER 9

Student Days

In September 1943 Lantie left Priors Ings and went away to college to be trained as a teacher. Long before this happened there were scenes and tantrums in the Prior's House as she protested against her fate.

"It isn't fair! I don't want to be a teacher. Why can't I leave school and get a job on a newspaper? I want to be a journalist."

"Nonsense!" snapped Mama. "You'll go to college and become qualified for a proper career. Newspapers indeed!"

"Why can't I go in the Forces? I want to join the Land Army and do some useful war work?" said Lantie piously.

This idea cause Poppa to laugh so much that the tears rolled down his cheeks. When he had recovered he said, "You wouldn't last five minutes in the Land Army, my love. Why, you don't even like gardening. You can't get up in the mornings unless Mama calls you half a dozen times. How could you rise at five or six o'clock on a cold winter's day to milk a herd of cows and drive a tractor?"

Lantie acknowledged the truth of this but she had often thought that she would look becoming in the smart jodhpurs and green jerseys worn by the young women who worked on the local farms.

The arguments went on and on for weeks. At last Mama became exasperated and put an end to the objections.

"I've heard the last word about it. You'll go to college whether you like it or not. You are too young and silly to realise that you need qualifications for a profession, but you will be thankful for them later in life. I won't hear another word on the matter. You will go to college." As an afterthought she added, "Your Poppa has set his heart on it and I won't have him disappointed."

Unlike Mama, who had been to a grammar school, Poppa had started work at fourteen. He was anxious that his children should have the chance of a higher education which had been denied to him.

Realising that further argument was useless, Lantie began to apply for admission to two or three colleges. Perverse as ever, she chose ones as far away from home as possible. She was called for an interview to the one at the top of her list and was accepted. This college was on the far side of the Pennines and involved three train journeys to get there.

The College authorities supplied lists of essential clothes and books which each student would need. For months Mama gathered together these items and the more mundane clothing such as stockings, socks and handkerchiefs. Clothing coupons were limited and all the family's allocation was commandeered to equip Lantie for college. Mama insisted that everything must be new.

Shoes were needed in abundance. Outdoor shoes and indoor shoes; heavy shoes suitable for walking and gardening; Wellington boots; plimsolls for PT; hockey boots and slippers were all bought and marked with name tapes.

Over a period of months, Mama stockpiled underwear, nightwear, a new dressing gown, dresses, skirts, jumpers, cardigans and coats. Some were bought and some were hand made.

As the pile of clothes mounted up, Lantie started to take an interest in the proceedings. It was, she thought, rather like gathering together a trousseau without the bother of a wedding and a husband.

Some clothes could not be purchased until she arrived at college. The short, bright blue tunics and matching knickers for Physical Training had to be made to measure. Similarly, the blue blazer with its heavy gold badge was ordered after the start of the college year.

Some of the books on the list were bought and others were borrowed from friends. The expense mounted as the weeks passed.

If Mama and Poppa were worried by the strain on their financial resources they did not mention it. The college fees were due at the beginning of each term.

One day, a few weeks before she was to depart, Lantie sought out Mama to ask her a favour.

"Can I have my hair permed? It will last a year."

Mama looked at her straight, lanky mop and decided it would be a good idea. She handed over twenty-five shillings and Lantie set off for the hairdresser. After three hours of being clamped and tugged into steel rollers and strung up to a fearsome machine near the ceiling, she emerged feeling very pleased with her frizzy locks. Poppa gently teased her and called her his little golliwog but she did not mind as she felt transformed.

Eventually Poppa's large trunk and the big suitcase which had accompanied him on his travels to Canada and the United States were brought down from the loft. They bore labels which showed his various destinations.

All was packed and the trunk was locked and sent ahead by rail to the college. Lantie followed it a week or so later.

Mama, Poppa and Than went with her to Priors Ings station. Mama wept a little as they bade her goodbye. Lantie got on the train with a feeling of foreboding. She leaned out of the carriage window and waved to them as they stood on the platform until she was carried out of sight.

The college was on the outskirts of a busy town. It was a collection of pleasant, red-bricked buildings, some of which were covered with ivy. The grounds were extensive and well kept and the whole aspect looked pleasing.

There were fewer than a hundred students, all female, in attendance during the war years. Some of them lived in the college hostel where each one had a room of her own. Others were accommodated in a detached building near the entrance to the grounds. This was known as College House and had been the residence of the Principal in pre-war days. The present incumbent had her rooms in the hostel.

A few students lived in lodgings in the town. These were the envy of the college residents for they had much more freedom. In the evenings they could come and go without too many restrictions, especially if they had a benevolent landlady.

The girls came from many different educational establishments: convents; co-educational schools; single sex schools; academies and grammar schools. Probably the only thing that most of them had in common when they arrived was an acquaintance with *Palgrave's Golden Treasury* and the *National Song Book*. These were to be found in schools the length and breadth of the country at that time.

There were a number of Welsh girls at the college and Lantie was fascinated by their lilting musical voices and different culture. She made friends with the owners of names like Glenys, Dilys, Megan and Mair. Sometimes she went to Welsh Chapels with them, as well as trying every other denomination in the town including the Salvation Army.

To ease the newcomers into College life there was a 'Mother and Daughter' system. Each First Year student had a 'mother' from the Second Year who acted as guide and friend. The mothers helped with problems and queries. In the hostel dining room, where the tables were set for eight places, mothers and daughters sat together. Thus, even if they did not meet during the day, there was always some contact at meal times.

Lantie's college mother was a vivacious, black-haired girl from South Wales. Her cheerfulness helped to raise Lantie's spirits during the first few weeks when she was bewildered by the routine, depressed by the discipline and racked with homesickness.

The discipline at the college was very strict. The students in the hostel and College House had to sign themselves in by seven o'clock each weekday evening in the winter time. Then the doors were locked and bolted. On Saturdays and Sundays they were allowed out until nine thirty. In summer these times were extended to nine o'clock during the week and ten o'clock at weekends.

The college timetables were arranged so that each day was as full as possible with the minimum of spare time. As well as lectures in the academic subjects such as English, History, Geography and Biology, there were Method lectures. Here the students were taught how to teach every subject they were likely to encounter in the schools, including Physical Training, Country Dancing, Handicrafts and Music.

Having decided during the first week of term whether they wanted to teach Infants, Juniors or Seniors, the First Years were divided up into groups and followed a course of lectures for their group. Lantie chose Juniors, not being enamoured of the idea of dealing with very small children or hulking fourteen-year-olds.

The students realised, quite quickly, that life was not going to be a matter of sitting in lecture rooms and making notes. Once a week there were Demonstration Lessons. Groups were taken to schools in the town and surrounding villages to gain practical experience in the classroom. On the first occasion the tutor in charge of the group gave a lesson. Then the students took it in turn to prepare and give a lesson in front of the tutor and the other members of the group. Afterwards, the lesson was dissected and criticised by the observers.

Knowing that her turn would come, nobody dared venture beyond mild suggestions and faint praise. It was left to the tutor to point out the glaring faults, the paucity of the material content, the poor presentation and the irritating mannerisms.

This ordeal paled into insignificance when the time came for the First Year students to go out on School Practice. Everyone had to spend three weeks during the Autumn Term, and again in the Spring

96

Term, in the local schools. Each student had to take charge of a class of forty or fifty children and practise non-existent skills on them.

School Practice meant no more cosy gossiping evenings in the Common Room for Lantie and her friends. They had to prepare lessons, write out notes, make work cards, apparatus and illustrations – the latter to adorn the classroom walls. The children's books had to be marked each time they did a piece of written work.

The lesson notes were kept in special files and had to follow a set pattern. Under the headline 'Introduction', the student had to indicate how the opening of the lesson was planned.

'Development' needed a longer explanation to show the main theme of the lesson in detail. Any pictures, charts, cards and apparatus and the way in which they would be used, came under this heading.

'Conclusion' had to show how the lesson would be rounded off and the objectives realised.

The final section was 'Criticism'. In the unlikely event of a student not having a visit from her tutor or the Principal or the Head Teacher of the school, she had to make an assessment of her own performance.

These notes were written for each lesson taken by the student during the three weeks of School Practice. Every Saturday morning the files had to be handed in to the tutor, who checked them carefully. They had to be collected on Sunday evening when verbal praise or criticism was meted out.

By the end of the School Practice most of the students were mentally and physically exhausted. They were glad to get back to the routine of lectures.

During the Summer Vacation all First Year students had to arrange to do teaching practice at schools near their homes. This was much more relaxing as there were only the head teachers and staff to please. Most of them were sympathetic and nobody returned to college without a glowing report.

The Final School Practice was in the Spring term of the second year and it lasted a month. Not only were the students subjected to constant visits from the tutors and the Principal but they had to undergo visits from His Majesty's School Inspectors. The result of these four weeks was a deciding factor as to whether one obtained a teaching certificate.

Bells and gongs ruled the students' lives during the week. Bells rang for the start of lectures in the morning. Gongs rang to summon them to meals. Bells rang for 'Silences' in the evenings. The first Silence lasted from six o'clock until seven thirty. During this time students were meant to be working in their rooms. A gong sounded for supper at seven forty-five after which there was another Silence from eight thirty to nine thirty.

At ten twenty-five, the lights were momentarily dimmed as a warning that all rooms must be in darkness in five minutes time. As each door had a glass fanlight above it, there was no possibility of leaving on a light. This would have shone into the corridor like a beacon to alert the member of staff on duty.

Even so it was possible to do work which had been left undone after Lights Out. A bedspread draped over the side of a bed enabled a student to lie underneath and scribble at an unfinished essay by the light of a candle, without a glimmer shining through the glass above the door. The wonder was that the hostel was never burned to the ground.

Other rules were broken quite frequently. To circumvent the early curfew, a friend would slip downstairs and open a window in the Common Room to let in a backslider. The Boot Room at the back of the hostel was a repository for Wellington boots and odds and ends. It was used for making cocoa and a latecomer, who had been signed in by a friend, could slip in from the garden through the unbolted door.

The Principal of the college lectured in Psychology. She was a highly neurotic woman of strange moods. Most of the students were terrified of her and a summons to her room usually meant trouble. No doubt she was anxious for the virtue of her young charges when she formulated rules to this end. No men, be they brothers or male relations, were allowed upstairs in the rooms under any circumstances. All visitors, especially male ones, must have their names entered in the Visitors Book. Students could invite guests for afternoon tea which was provided in the Staff Dining room. The door must remain open if the guest or guests were male. The door was invariably closed.

As well as controlling the girls' lives inside the college, the Principal tried to extend her influence to their outside activities. The town was full of American troops and many of them were billeted in the Old Hall, a large country house not far from the main gates of the college.

The girls were forbidden to speak to the soldiers. "Remember, young ladies, that if an American soldier stops you to ask the time or for directions to somewhere you must walk on as if you have not heard. There will be no fraternisation."

In spite of this injunction a few friendships were formed with the Americans. It was not the ruling but the early curfews which effectively nipped in the bud any blossoming relationships. The G.I.s found it incredible that young women had to be indoors by nine thirty on a summer evening.

It was impossible to attend a dance in the town when the Saturday deadline was ten o'clock. Visits to the cinema were arranged in the afternoon, sometimes by skipping a lecture or two.

"It's like living in a nunnery," fumed Lantie and her friends. "Even Cinderella was allowed out until midnight."

There was no wonder that the students in the hostel and College House envied those who lived in lodgings. They lived far more interesting social lives after lecture hours.

The tutors at the college were mainly female, middle aged or elderly academics, who did their best to impart knowledge and method to the future educators of the nation. In Lantie's first year there were three older men who took Music, Art and Biology.

Some of the tutors had affectionate nicknames which probably dated back many years. 'Mickie' was a strong, forceful woman who lectured in History. She was kind and well liked in spite of her brusque manner. She was large and stately and moved about the college 'like a ship in full sail' as someone described her.

Mickie's students were kept enthralled by her narrative style and she brought the dullest patches of history to life. After imparting some ribald facts about an historical figure, she would say, "Now my dears, we must leave the Byways of Scandal and return to the Highways of History."

She was a great advocate of good discipline in the classroom. One of her favourite stories related to her going to visit a student on School Practice and finding the class in uproar.

"'Stop!!' I bellowed and the noise ceased at once. 'Now get back to your desks'. The poor girl was in tears but she pulled herself together and took the lesson. Afterwards I had a few words with her. 'My dear,' I said, 'the first and most important thing you must do is to make the children obey you. If they are climbing up the walls and going out through the windows, it is your duty to bring them down and get them back into their places. Never mind if you don't teach a thing all the lesson. Make them behave and then the teaching will be easy'."

'Trom' was a gentle, self-effacing person who lectured in Handicrafts. Whenever anyone was stuck for an idea as to what to do with a piece of weaving or embroidery, she would suggest, diffidently "How about a jolly little pochette?"

The craft syllabus called for more than jolly pochettes and all her students had to produce garments, both knitted and sewn, items of leatherwork, weaving, embroidery and canework. This was not an easy subject for Lantie and she had to enlist Mama's help during the vacations in order to finish off some of her offerings.

'Doc', an eccentric, middle aged man, specialised in Biology and Gardening and was very popular with the students. As part of their war effort everyone had to do a number of hours work each week in the gardens. Lantie decided that it might as well be one of her subjects as she had to do the work in any case.

A number of allotments had been created in the grounds by previous gardening students and the produce was used in the college kitchen. Lantie was fortunate during the first year as Doc chose her plot for his demonstrations. He showed the group how to double dig, make a celery trench, hoe, rake, sow seeds and transplant cuttings. By the end of the year she had the best plot in the garden.

It was a different story during the second year. Doc left and his place was taken by a woman lecturer who did not use anyone's plot for demonstrations but told everyone what they must do.

Owing to the difficulties of travelling in wartime, the girls were allowed to go home only one weekend each term. A few, who lived only a short bus or train ride away, were able to visit their families for a day at the weekends.

It was half term before Lantie went home to Priors Ings. Nobody, not even Mama nor the College Principal, seemed to have any qualms about young women travelling on dimly lit, blacked out trains packed with troops. Often Lantie spent the long, slow journeys in crowded corridors, sitting on some soldier's kitbag and exchanging backchat with half-a-dozen uniformed males.

When she arrived home for her first half term she felt as changed as if she had been living on another planet. She looked out of the carriage window as the train pulled into Priors Ings station and saw Mama, Poppa and Than waiting on the platform. A feeling of relief and affection swept over her when she realised that they were exactly the same as when she left them a few weeks earlier.

They hugged and kissed her and they walked down the lane to the Prior's House, all talking at once. Uncle Tobias was in the kitchen and he plied her with questions as soon as she went to greet him. After all her homesickness it was wonderful to be back and to know that nothing had changed. She felt loved and secure and a world away from the routine of college.

In spite of the fact that Lantie was growing fat on the stodgy college diet, Mama was convinced that she was on the verge of starvation. Each week she sent her a food parcel containing cakes, a fatless sponge, home made jam and any other delicacies she could spare. One week she used her own coupons and the alternate one she used Uncle Tobias's rations to buy sweets to send to Lantie. In addition there was a letter and a ten shilling note which was her weekly pocket money.

The college food was wholesome but dull. The rations were supplemented by vegetables from the garden and stodgy puddings, such as jam roly poly, nicknamed Dead Baby, Spotted Dick and a pastry concoction call Fly Pie. These were accompanied by white sauces or anaemic yellow custards.

The butter ration at that time was two ounces a week. Each girl had a small covered dish which contained her allocation. Lantie divided her little slab into sections to make it last for six days. One day a week a ration of margarine appeared and the girl sitting at the head of the table divided it carefully into eight minute squares.

All the girls moaned about the food and held the Matron-cum-Housekeeper responsible for their monotonous diet. She was nick-named 'Horace' and was suspected of feeding the staff far better than the students. She was a very bossy woman and, because she dined in the Staff room, she considered herself an academic rather than a domestic.

Horace was always around, checking on the students and asking questions. She was suspected of carrying tales to the Principal.

"How else," demanded one indignant girl, "did her Ladyship know I was talking to an American in the town? Because Horace passed us and by the time I got back there was a message for me to go down the corridor and explain myself. Nobody but Horace could have told her. Madam was livid and threatened to send me down if it happened again. Surely you can't be sent down for talking to an American soldier?"

One Sunday evening the doors had been locked and bolted when a girl arrived late and had to ring the bell. Horace answered the door,

"Where have you been?" she demanded.

"To Church. The sermon went on a long time and the vicar and his wife asked me in for a coffee."

As she was not the sort of girl who was likely to be gallivanting off with Americans, she was admitted.

"Why didn't you go to church this morning?" asked Horace.

"I did. I went this afternoon as well," came the reply.

"What! Three times a day! Do you think God has nothing else to do except listen to you three times a day? Off to your room at once, Miss."

The war scarcely impinged upon the lives of the girls at college. The only newspaper in the Common Room was a double-paged provincial sheet in which invasions and battles vied for space with accounts of Council Meetings and local activities.

As a concession to the state of hostilities a fire-watching rota was in force and two students spent the night in the building where the lectures were held. This was separate from the hostel and it was a cold, creepy place in the winter time. Fortunately the duty did not come round too often as members of the staff took their turns.

Those on duty would collect a tray of food from the kitchen, usually sandwiches and rock buns, and set out through the grounds carrying gas masks and rugs and wearing as many layers of clothing as seemed necessary. Once inside the building they locked the doors behind them and made their way along the echoing corridors to the fire watching room. They locked this door and then settled down to make tea or cocoa and to eat their supper.

In the event of an air raid they were supposed to protect the building by spotting fires. Sleep was not easy as the creaks and noises of the empty rooms were very audible. Yet most of the fire watchers managed to doze off and, happily, their resourcefulness and services were never put to the test.

As well as fire watching, the students were formed into fire fighting teams and were obliged to practise with hoses and stirrup pumps using water from large tanks strategically placed in the grounds. These rehearsals were more occasions for hilarity than serious attempts at dousing incendiary bombs.

Although they were situated away from a war zone, air raid practices were often held at the college. During the day, if the signal, the continual ringing of a bell, was given, the students left whatever they were doing and assembled in the grounds. At night they were roused from their beds by the same sustained bell-ringing and by members of the staff banging on their doors. Then they had to make their way to the ground floor, dressed in warm clothing and carrying rugs and gas masks.

On one occasion they were sitting on the floor of the corridors and answering the roll call when it was discovered that Lantie's friend, Cynthia, was missing. A member of the staff went up to the top floor and to her room at the far end. There, in spite of bells, alarms, knocking on doors and general noise, Cynthia was sleeping peacefully.

That was one of the few times when the alarm was a real one. The town had been alerted because a crippled American bomber with bombs on board was circling the area on automatic pilot, the crew having baled out. Where it eventually crashed was never disclosed.

The kind of war work which was often over-subscribed was the Saturday night and Sunday Canteen Duty at the busy railway station in the town. It was amazing that the Principal allowed this activity, but it appeared she was over-persuaded by a friend on the local Education Committee who suggested that her young ladies could do this vital war work.

The young ladies in question nearly fell over each other to put their names on the Canteen Duty List. Saturday nights were the most popular as it meant staying away from the hostel overnight. The duty lasted from ten o'clock until seven o'clock on the Sunday morning.

In reality the work was far from glamorous. Members of the WVS cooked the food and the students were there to take orders, fetch and carry, wash the dishes and do the general skivvying.

At intervals throughout the night, troop trains would pull into the station and disgorge their occupants. Soldiers, sailors and airmen poured into the canteen and stood three or four deep at the counters, shouting their orders.

"Beans on toast and tea, Miss."

"Eggs and chips and coffee."

"Beans, chips and eggs, please."

"Hey miss, these aren't my beans. I ordered egg on toast."

By the time they were all served and the money had been taken, the canteen began to empty. The dirty dishes had to be collected and washed. Hardly was this done when another train load of men would arrive. Real chaos ensued when two trains came in together.

By four o'clock in the morning the girls were exhausted and were counting the hours to when the Sunday relief team arrived. Make-up had long since melted in the heat, leaving them with shiny noses, straggly hair and aching legs. Their stomachs felt queasy from the smell of food.

"I don't think I can face serving another helping of baked beans with anything," moaned Lantie, but she did.

About five o'clock in the morning, after drinking coffee and eating toast, minus beans or eggs, which were of the dried and scrambled variety, they got a new lease of life. They realised that Canteen Duty was not the environment from which romances grew. It was sheer hard work, yet Lantie and her friends volunteered again and again, just for the novelty of being away from the confines of the college.

There was one other occasion when the First Year students were allowed out during curfew. The Principal decided that they must attend a series of lectures by a local lady doctor on the subject of Sex Education.

The girls were divided into groups and they went on different nights of the week during the Autumn Term. Lantie and her group set off into the town full of expectation and interest.

The lady doctor was large and formidable. However, what they learned from her on the subject of sex could be found in any text book. Sometimes she seemed to forget they were students and spoke as if she was addressing an ante-natal class.

"You should always use a chamber pot. It helps to spread the hips and enlarge the pelvis. All my four daughters have been trained from babyhood to use a chamber pot. Now they have good wide hips ready for easy child bearing. Any questions?" The girls gazed up at her and, for once, they were all speechless.

After the summer vacation, the First Years became the Second Years and had the responsibility of 'daughters' of their own. Ahead of them loomed Final School Practice and Final Examinations.

During the Autumn term these seemed a long way off and like the proverbial cricket, some, Lantie among them, gossiped and laughed around the Common Room fire each evening.

It was during this period that Lantie wanted a weekend leave in order to attend the wedding of a close friend. She asked if she could leave on Friday after lunch. Permission was refused as she had lectures on the Friday afternoon and Saturday morning.

"You can go after lectures on Saturday," decreed the Principal.

"But the wedding is on Saturday morning," said Lantie in dismay.

"Then you will have to miss it. After all, it is not as if it is a member of your family who is getting married."

"But – - – - -," began Lantie.

"I have no more to say on the matter. Goodnight."

Lantie was determined to go to the wedding and arranged for two or three friends to cover her absence in case of an air raid warning or an unexpected fire practice. As everyone had to attend the Saturday morning lectures, she knew she would not be missed in the crowd.

Around midnight her close friend, Cynthia, whose room was at the end of the top corridor next to the fire escape, unbolted the door and let her out on to the iron staircase. She stood still for a moment until her eyes became accustomed to the darkness. She heard Cynthia rebolt the door. Then she crept quietly down the fire escape with her shoes in one hand and a small travelling bag in the other.

The fire escape went past the Principal's bedroom but once that obstacle was cleared Lantie soon reached the bottom of the stairs. She put on her shoes and made her way through the dark grounds. When she emerged on to the road she turned to her right and began to walk along the straight road which led to the town. This road was known as Coll Straits and there were fields and hedges on either side but no dwellings apart from Old Hall.

As Lantie drew level with the gates of the big house, which was on the opposite side of the road, there was a sudden noise. Two black American soldiers on sentry duty sprang to attention. All she could see were the whites of their eyes and their brilliant white teeth as they grinned at her.

With a squeak of fright she started to run. Behind her she heard the loud laughter and ribald remarks of the two guards. She did not stop running until she got to the station, where it took her several minutes to get her breath.

Mama and Poppa were pleased that she was able to get to the wedding and it was a happy occasion. Nevertheless they were shocked when they learned that she had come without permission.

"What if you have been found out? You will be expelled! Oh! the disgrace of it," said Mama

When Lantie arrived back at the college on the Sunday evening she found that all was well. Her friends had covered her absence and her misdeed was never discovered.

Final School Practice lasted four weeks and was a nightmare for all concerned. It was followed by the practical examinations in subjects as diverse as Gardening, Handicrafts and Music.

On the day of the Gardening Practical it poured with rain. The students huddled together in the Potting Shed and waited until they were sent for one by one.

Lantie stood beside her plot, feeling damp and depressed. The examiner was a middle-aged man who looked cross and sounded impatient.

"What's the matter with your broad beans, girl?" he barked.

Lantie said she didn't know there was anything the matter with them.

"Oh, they're only smothered with black fly. Nothing to worry about, eh? How far apart would you plant brussel sprouts?"

"A foot?" she hazarded. "Two feet?"

"Go and get what you need and let me see you plant a row of parsnips," he commanded.

Lantie dashed through the rain to the Potting Shed where the other examinees waited.

"What do I need to plant parsnip seed? How far apart shall I plant them?" She snatched up a ball of string, two markers and a dibber and returned to her plot.

"Hmmm," was all the examiner said when she had finished planting the seeds.

"Now, young woman, just rack your brains and tell me to what disease carrots are prone."

"Carrot fly," replied Lantie beaming at him.

"Huh! You're getting brilliant, aren't you?" came the riposte.

Evidently her written work, in the form of a gardening journal, made up for her shortcomings in the practical examination because she passed in gardening.

This caused Poppa much amusement and years later he would ask her to do some task in the garden, saying, "You can do it, my love. You have a qualification in gardening on your certificate".

The war in Europe was over by the time Lantie and her fellow students had finished their training. They took their Final written examinations and after two years of strict discipline, much grumbling and a great deal of laughter, their college life was over. They would not know until the end of July whether they had passed.

In the meantime there was a quota system through which Local Education Authorities accepted a number of newly qualified teachers to do a year's probationary service before their certificates were ratified. Lantie and her friend Cynthia were posted to Liverpool and they agreed that they would find lodgings together.

Before dismissing them the Principal, in her final address, referred to the Education Act of 1944. One of the many provisions had raised the starting salary of teachers to two hundred and fifty pounds a year.

"Two hundred and fifty pounds," she said, almost sorrowfully. "I feel certain very, very few of you are worth all that amount of money."

No doubt she was right.

During the two years at college, groups of friends formed and reformed, partly influenced by the subjects they studied, the different schools at which they had practised and their various interests. Yet some of the friendships made during these years lasted a lifetime.

Lantie and six of her closest friends were still having an annual reunion fifty years after their student days. All of them stayed in the teaching profession. They followed the principles and methods they had learned in college. They aimed to turn the charges in their care into literate, numerate, well behaved children. When they retired they were replaced by others with different methods and ideas.

Sometimes when she looked back, Lantie felt that the friendships she made in college were the only lasting things of value that had survived down the years.

CHAPTER 10

Liverpool

It was August when Cynthia and Lantie arrived in Liverpool to start their year as probationer teachers. They lodged with a middle aged woman in a quiet suburban road. The only other resident in the house was an elderly male lodger of a taciturn disposition.

On the first day of term the two girls set off for school in different directions. Cynthia had to walk to the East Lancashire Road and catch a tram which took her into the city. Lantie walked through the nearby park to her school.

This discrepancy in their journeys was due to the fact that Mama had insisted on helping to find them accommodation. Armed with a list of addresses supplied by the Education Office, she and Lantie had surveyed several possibilities in the area of Lantie's school. None of them was judged to be suitable by Mama. Finally she came upon their present lodgings. She looked at the rooms, interviewed the landlady and went back to Priors Ings well pleased with her day's work.

Lantie walked through the school gates before half past eight in the morning. There were a few children in the playground and one of them took her into the building and went to fetch the caretaker. He directed her to the Staff Room which was two floors up, access being by a stone staircase.

"Nobody's here yet," he said. "They won't be long because they have to sign the book at twenty to nine. Miss Brown'll be here first an' she has to cross the Mersey from Wallasey."

Lantie sat down in the Staff Room and waited. Soon she heard footsteps and voices.

"Would you believe? I haven't heard a word from that stupid probationer, not a word."

The stupid probationer quaked in her shoes.

Two women came into the Staff Room. One, who turned out to be the Head Mistress, Miss Brown, was a short, stout lady with grey hair which was swept up into a bun. She had a pleasant, kindly face, but at that moment she wore a cross expression. Her companion was Miss Forbes, the deputy head.

"Oh! I suppose you are the probationer," said Miss Brown, catching sight of Lantie. "Why on earth didn't you get in touch with me, you silly girl? How can I organise your work if I don't know anything about you?"

Lantie managed to interrupt her flow of words. "I did write to you. I wrote as soon as the Authority sent me the name of the school."

She was ushered out of the Staff Room and into Miss Brown's room. The Head riffled through a pile of mail on her desk and was slightly mollified to find Lantie's letter. She bade her sit down and began to talk to her about the class to which she had been assigned.

Outside in the playground a whistle was blown by the teacher on duty and the children stood still. After a second whistle they formed into lines. At a signal they filed quietly into school and to their classes.

Miss Brown took Lantie to a classroom and introduced her to her pupils, a class of forty-nine ten year old girls. Then she handed over a register and told her to mark it carefully.

Fortunately the teacher's desk was of the old fashioned type with a step up to a small platform and a fixed seat with a back rest. From here she had a good view of the whole classroom and this gave her a measure of confidence.

The day was spent in sorting and giving out reading and exercise books. There were composition books, spelling books, arithmetic books; books for tables, books for Nature Study, History and Geography. Each child had to put her name and the subject on the front of the books. Reading books, graded and in sets, were distributed by calling the girls one at a time to her desk and hearing them read a passage.

Meanwhile the class was not allowed to remain idle. The children had to write a composition entitled "My Holiday". When this was finished they were told to write their tables, starting at the two times. This work was done on loose paper.

Miss Brown came in several times during the day and gave instructions on various matters. She reminded Lantie that, even though the children's work was not done in their exercise books that day, it must be marked and returned to them.

"Remember, every single piece of work must be marked. The children must know that you are aware of everything they do. Otherwise they will become slack and untidy if they think you aren't bothering to mark their books. I shall come in and inspect all work from time to time."

Playtime came and went and dinner time arrived with Lantie still in a muddle. Miss Brown sent someone to tell her to come for her lunch. She picked up her handbag and a packet of sandwiches and followed the monitor to the Staff Room. Here she was introduced to four other teachers and she spent the lunch hour being quizzed in a probing but friendly manner.

The afternoon session was as chaotic as the morning had been, but by the end of the day she had a timetable to guide her for the rest of the week. It was with relief that she dismissed the class at four o'clock.

Lantie returned to the lodgings in a state of exhaustion. The landlady was busy in the kitchen so she sat in the front parlour and waited for Cynthia to arrive. She came back in a similar state of weariness and they discussed the day's events while they waited for their evening meal.

To their surprise the supper was served very early. When they had eaten it, the landlady came into the dining room wearing her outdoor clothes.

"I have to leave for work at six o'clock," she said. "Perhaps you will be good enough to give Mr. Palfrey his supper. He doesn't get back here until half past six.'

When Mama had asked if she was at home all day, she had replied truthfully that she was. She did not add that she worked as an usherette in one of the city theatres each weekday evening.

"Now all you need to do is to take his dinner out of the oven, remove the top plate and give it to him. The sweet is on the kitchen table. Most nights it will be cold sweet unless I make a milk pudding." These instructions indicated that she expected the girls to do this chore every evening.

Mr. Palfrey was not a conversationalist but was amiable enough. It seemed to be his habit to wash and change as soon as he came in. When he had eaten his meal, he got up and said he was going out to his club.

"Did he say club or pub?" asked Cynthia after he had gone.

"I expect it means the same thing, whichever he said," replied Lantie.

They cleared the table and washed the dishes. Then they went into the sitting room to prepare their lessons for the next day.

Gradually Lantie sorted out her work and got to know the children. The days became less chaotic and Miss Brown was very helpful and sympathetic.

"I know it is all very confusing and worrying at first but you will soon learn to cope," she said kindly.

One morning, during the second week of term, she took over the class while Lantie sat at the back. Using only the blackboard and a piece of chalk she gave a lesson, the equal of which Lantie had never seen, either on School Practice or College Demonstration lessons. The children listened intently and answered her questions sensibly. Before she directed them to do their written work she said, "Now we cannot all be clever because we are all different. However, we can all do neat, tidy work and keep our writing books looking beautiful. That is what I want to see, neat, tidy work."

Lantie felt she would never be as good a teacher as Miss Brown, and she was very conscious of her shortcomings. The Head laughed and said, "Don't worry, my dear. I've had years and years of practice. You'll turn out all right in the end."

At the lodgings the two girls were getting more and more resentful at having to look after Mr. Palfrey in the evenings. When he went out they had a great deal of preparation to do for school. They did not like answering the door bell to callers. They would go down the hall together, one of them carrying a poker, in case the callers turned out to be intruders.

"I'm fed up of giving him his supper and washing the dishes," fumed Cynthia. "We are paying her to look after us, she is not paying us to look after him."

"Let's go out tomorrow night and see what happens," said Lantie. "We'll go and visit Norah."

Norah was a college friend who lived with her family in a pleasant house beyond the city boundaries. During their student days, Cynthia and Lantie had gone home with her on several occasions. Her parents were very hospitable and they were always warmly welcomed.

"Yes! We'll go out and see Norah tomorrow night," agreed Cynthia.

After supper the next evening they got up from the table before the landlady had time to put on her coat and hat.

114

"We're going out and we don't know what time we shall be back. May we have a key, please?" said Lantie.

The woman looked as if she had been struck.

"Where are you going?" she demanded.

"That's our business," retorted Cynthia.

She recovered herself and said, "You can't have a key. I haven't a spare one."

"Then we shall have to make sure we come back after you," said Lantie.

They had a pleasant evening with Norah and arrived back about midnight. The landlady let them in without a word. They bade her goodnight and went upstairs. The next night she handed them a key to share between them.

From that time onwards they went out two or three evenings a week and at the weekends. Sometimes it was to a theatre, a concert or a dance at one of the restaurants in the city.

A month later the landlady delivered her counter attack.

"You will have to find somewhere else to live. I've got two gentlemen lodgers coming and I shall need your room."

"But where shall we go?" asked Lantie, somewhat shaken.

"I'll ask one or two women who were on the Billeting Officer's list. There's one with a big house in Queen's Drive. Maybe she will have you. I'm more comfortable looking after gentleman lodgers. I'm not used to young women who are out all hours of the night."

Cynthia and Lantie wondered who would give the newcomers their supper. They had a few days of worry until they were told of two vacancies at a house in Queen's Drive. They were to go there on Saturday morning to be inspected.

The house to which the girls were directed was large and imposing. They rang the bell on the door of the porch and waited. Within a few moments they heard an inner door being opened and the front door was flung back.

A large smiling woman with beautiful auburn hair stood in the doorway. Before they had time to speak she stood aside and beckoned them indoors.

"Come in, come in, I've been expecting you. I'm Mrs. Willow but everyone calls me Ma."

They followed her through the entrance porch and into a hall. There were several doors leading off from here and she led them through one of them into a large room. "Sit down, my dears. Would you like a cup of tea or coffee?"

They were too anxious to get on with the business in hand to accept her offer. Sensing this she stood up and went to the door. "Perhaps you would like to go upstairs and see the room? Then we can have a chat and you can go off and talk things over."

They went upstairs and were shown a large bedroom which was next door to a bathroom. There seemed to be numerous other rooms on that floor of the house. Returning downstairs they all sat in the living room.

Hesitantly Lantie asked about the terms. "Would twenty-five shillings a week be about right?" asked Ma.

The girls looked at each other and said it would. That was what they were paying at their present lodgings.

"Of course, that would include a cooked breakfast and dinner at night and a packed lunch. I will do all your washing so you needn't send anything out. Perhaps you would like to go away and talk it over?"

Cynthia and Lantie did not need to talk it over. They looked at each other and nodded. "Yes, we'll take the room," they said together.

"Good! It will be lovely to have young ladies in the house," said Ma, looking pleased. "There's my husband and my two sons. One of them, Tom, is married and he and his wife, Nan, and their little girl have rooms here. Then I have two other guests, both men. When would you like to move in?"

"Would this afternoon be convenient?" asked Cynthia.

Ma seemed delighted and insisted that they had a cup of tea. Before they left to go back and gather their belongings she gave each of them a door key.

So the girls moved into Ma Willow's house and into the lives of the people who lived there.

Every morning Ma wakened them with cups of tea. By the time they came downstairs she had cooked their breakfasts and put their bags and packed lunches on chairs in the hall, ready for their departure.

When Lantie crept back from school, worn and weary, Ma would jump up from her armchair by the fire and make her sit down while she brewed fresh tea and offered a selection of cakes. "These will put you on until we have dinner," she said.

Half an hour later, Cynthia arrived home and she was treated in like manner. They both sat and drank tea and gossiped while Ma cooked the evening meal.

During the weekend after they had moved in the girls met Pop, Ma's husband, her elder son and his family, her younger son Jim and the two male lodgers.

On the Monday evening when they had had their meal, they heard the porch door bang and someone came through the hall. A young woman appeared round the living room door. Ma, who was relaxing with a cup of tea after her culinary exertions, introduced the newcomer.

"This is Beryl, Jim's young lady." The girl was tall and slim with lovely, dark curly hair.

"Hi," she said, in reply to the introductions.

Ma brought her a cup of tea and she sat down to chat. After a while Jim came in from the garage and said "Hi." They exchanged a few words and he returned from whence he came.

"It's the Big End on the bench tonight," Ma confided to them all.

The second great love of Jim's life was his motorbike. He spent several evenings a week taking it to pieces, cleaning, tuning, mending and getting it in order so that he and Beryl could go out at weekends. Both of them were fond of dancing and they used to travel to various social gatherings on Friday and Saturday nights.

About ten o'clock, Jim came through from the garage and into the kitchen to divest of oil and grease. After he had been upstairs to wash and change, they had coffee and biscuits and then he walked Beryl home.

When she was not attending Evening Classes to further her education, she would bring her knitting and sit in Ma's living room chatting to anyone who happened to be there. This was Lantie, more often than not, as Cynthia, being a very attractive young woman, had far more boy friends.

As a result Beryl and Lantie became close friends. They had a similar sense of humour and would go off into peals of laughter that sometimes bordered on hysteria. After Lantie had left Liverpool and when both had married they remained in touch. Eventually Beryl and Jim emigrated to Canada but the friendship stretched down the years and across thousands of miles.

During their first week at the house the girls sampled Ma's excellent cooking. "Scouse tonight, girls. I hope you like it."

"Scouse? What's scouse?" they asked. Ma's husband, Pop, came in at that moment.

"Do you mean to tell me you don't know what scouse is? And you call yourselves teachers?"

"Don't tease them," scolded Ma. "It's a sort of hash but special to Liverpool you see. Everybody calls it scouse."

"Yes," said Pop, "and all good Liverpudlians are called scouses too."

Cynthia and Lantie had not been at Ma Willow's very long when their social lives began to flourish. Several boy friends appeared on the scene through connections of distant cousins, brothers of friends and friends of friends.

They went out with them during the week and at weekends to theatres, to dinners at some of the new restaurants that had appeared in the city at the end of the war and to concerts in the Philharmonic Hall. At that time few young men had cars, consequently the girls were often escorted to the tram stop in the city centre and left to travel home by themselves. Sometimes they were together and sometimes alone but neither of them had any sense of fear, even at midnight.

The worst danger to which Lantie was exposed, on one occasion, was listening to a group of sailors singing an unabridged version of 'Maggie Mae' as the tram rattled along the East Lancashire Road. She used to alight at the tram stop and walk along the deserted Queen's Drive to Ma's house.

There was always someone about however late the girls arrived home. Ma went to bed early, tired out after a long, hard day but Pop or Jim were usually around.

"Yer whacker isn't back yet. Want a cup of tea?" Pop would say, if Lantie arrived home first. She had discovered that the Liverpudlian term 'whacker' meant friend.

Had either of the girls failed to arrive on the last tram, someone would have been aware of it and the alarm would have been raised. They were not conscious of this discreet surveillance.

At school Lantie was getting into the routine of work. She had to be in her classroom by eight forty each morning after signing the book in Miss Brown's room. As a probationer she was excused playground duty but was expected to stay in her room during this time and prepare for the next lessons. A monitor brought her coffee and collected the empty cup as the children returned from their playtime.

One day, to her surprise, Miss Brown came in carrying a cup of coffee. She put it down on a desk and turned to Lantie. "Now I know you will think I am an interfering old woman, but I must ask you not to wear lipstick while you are on the school premises. It gets on to the cups and sets a bad example to the monitors. They are eleven years old and at an impressionable age."

Lantie meekly agreed to forego her lipstick. She learned, years later, that her successor was not so docile. It appeared that she was asked not to come to school wearing a headscarf.

"Why not?" demanded the young woman.

"Because you look like a factory girl," replied Miss Brown.

"And what is wrong with factory girls?" asked the headscarf wearer.

"Nothing, but they are not on my staff. I insist that you come to school dressed in a suitable manner," came Miss Brown's heated retort. As the young teacher continued to wear a headscarf there was a certain amount of friction between them for the remainder of her stay at the school.

Whatever stresses and strains they had at work, Cynthia and Lantie were thoroughly spoiled by Ma. Neither girl made her bed or tidied the room because Ma did it for them. She cleaned their shoes, washed and ironed their clothes and brought them breakfast to bed on Saturdays and Sundays. There was no wonder that they loved her.

When Lantie went home to Priors Ings at half term or the school holidays, Mama was vexed by her lazy, sluttish ways. She was at her wits' end to understand such idleness. She did not realise that, in Liverpool, the two girls were getting a unique service for only twenty-five shillings a week.

Pop Willow owned a motorbike and sidecar. Like Jim, he spent a lot of time in the garage with parts of his vehicle distributed along the bench. When it was in one piece, Ma used to squeeze herself into the sidecar and they would go out for the evening.

One night he was telling the girls about the marvels of the Mersey Tunnel.

"You mean to say you've never been through the tunnel? You don't know what you've missed! I'll take you there one afternoon at the weekend."

The following Sunday Cynthia and Lantie gathered round Pop's motorbike. One of them clambered into the sidecar and the other sat on the pillion and clutched him tightly. Ma came out with an extra rug for the sidecar and to make sure they were both well wrapped up against the cold. With their hair streaming behind them they went on an exhilarating ride through the bomb scarred streets of Liverpool and down into the tunnel. The lights blazed overhead and the traffic speeded along beside them.

On the other side of the river Pop stopped his machine so that they could change places in the sidecar and pillion before they raced back again. Ma had tea ready for them when they arrived. She beamed with pleasure as she listened to their enthusiastic accounts of the journey.

Although Ma spoiled the girls, she was careful to keep an eye on their social activities. In 'loco parentis' she insisted on inspecting their boy friends. "Bring him to tea on Sunday and I'll give him the once over," she would say.

Numerous acquaintances were given hospitality and winnowed by her experienced eye.

"He seems a bit wild, that one."

"Not much about him, has he dear?" she would remark in her forthright way.

Yet in many ways she was very liberal and easy going.

"Oh, it's dancing the light fantastic tonight is it? Go and enjoy yourself while you can, dear. I used to love dancing when I was young but Pop never cared for it."

Mama would have been horrified had she known that, around the time the family at the Prior's House were settling down to their nightly cocoa, Lantie was on a tram heading for the bright lights of Liverpool.

After some months, Cynthia acquired a steady boy friend. He was a naval officer and used to come to the house to call for her and always escorted her home again. They went out quite often during the week and at the weekends.

Lantie, meanwhile had had two or three escorts but none was to her liking.

"Why is it they want to be serious before you've known them five minutes?" she grumbled to Ma. "It puts me off when they start talking about engagement rings. I don't want to be married for years and years, if ever."

"Oh, you haven't met Mr. Right yet, darling," soothed Ma.

After dinner one summer's evening Lantie was sitting curled up on the window seat in the living room, gazing moodily into the tree lined road. Cynthia had gone to their bedroom to get ready to go out.

Into view on the other side of the road came Cynthia's young man accompanied by a khaki clad figure. Within a couple of minutes there was a knock on the door and the two of them entered. Peter, the naval officer, introduced his friend, whose name was Nick, to Ma and Lantie. The former bustled out to get them cups of coffee.

Lantie looked at the stranger without much interest. He was very tall with fair curly hair and a deep tan.

"What regiment are you in?" asked Ma, settling back into her armchair.

"I'm in the Royal Marine Commandos," he replied.

Lantie gathered from the conversation that he had recently returned from overseas.

"Er, Lantie – – –" began Peter, "are you doing anything this evening?"

"Why?" she asked suspiciously.

"Well, I thought – – – he thought – – we – –."

"Do you want to come out with me?" interrupted Nick.

"Where?" she asked, looking him up and down.

"Anywhere you like. The theatre, or a dance?"

"It's too late to get tickets for a theatre and I'm not in the mood for dancing," she replied.

"Well, we can find somewhere. Do you or don't you want to come?" The young man sounded irritated.

"Why don't you go out darling. A change will do you good," interjected Ma.

At that moment Cynthia came into the room and Ma paused to admire her appearance. She had a natural flair for clothes which Lantie envied but never managed to emulate. On this occasion her blonde hair was in a neat page boy style, her make-up was perfect and her dress showed her slim figure.

She and Peter departed and the conversation with the marine resumed.

"Are you coming out or aren't you?" he demanded. "I'm not sitting here all night waiting for you to make up your mind."

"Oh, all right," Lantie got down from the window seat and started towards the door.

"Hurry up," he said.

She gave him a filthy look and flounced out of the room. At that time she was quite unaware that she had met her future husband.

Miss Brown spent a lot of time during the summer term preparing Lantie for the visit of His Majesty's Inspectors. Their favourable verdict was necessary for her teaching certificate to be ratified. If she failed to come up to their standards she would have to spend another year as a probationer teacher.

When the Inspectors arrived they sat at the back of the classroom and made notes. They examined the children's books and looked at the illustrations on the walls and the models and apparatus on the tables.

After the children had gone home, Miss Brown came bustling in, all smiles, to announce that the Inspectors had been very pleased and she had passed.

"I'm not supposed to tell you because you will be informed officially, but I thought you would want to know that all is well."

Later that week Miss Brown offered Lantie a permanent post on the staff. "Better the devil you know," she laughed as Lantie accepted.

Nonetheless, her days in Liverpool were numbered. Cynthia did not return after the summer holidays and Lantie was very lonely without her. Sometimes she went to visit Norah and her family where she was always sure of a warm welcome. Beryl came during the week but she had little incentive to go out on her own.

"You don't have to stay in and mope because that young man of yours has gone abroad," scolded Ma. "Come out with Pop and me." So, occasionally she clambered on Pop's pillion and with Ma in the sidecar they roared away to the White Swan.

One day when she arrived home from school, she found three young sailors ensconced in the living room. The Billeting Officer had called and Ma had been over-persuaded to take them in.

They were a lively trio and Lantie had many discussions and arguments with them. One evening when Beryl was at her typing class, the sailors taught Lantie to play pontoon and other card games.

With beginner's luck she won small sums of money from each of them. After that they were chary when she suggested a game of cards.

As the term wore on she decided to give in her notice and go home to Priors Ings. Miss Brown was upset but not surprised. "The children will miss you and I shall be sorry to lose you. Now I shall have to start all over again with someone else."

Lantie shed a few tears on her last day at school but she wept more copiously on Ma's ample bosom.

"Never mind, darling. You know you can come back here at any time," said Ma, dabbing her own eyes.

She carried Lantie's case to the tram stop and waved as the tram rattled her away on her journey to Lime Street and the station.

The change from city life to the quietness of Priors Ings was traumatic. The family suffered from Lantie's incessant grumbles with varying degrees of patience. Many times she threatened to pack her bags and return to Liverpool, but they remained unpacked. As she had suffered from homesickness and pined for the Prior's House during her early weeks at college, so she longed to be back in the warm, uncritical presence of Ma Willow.

Thirty years later, when Ma went to Canada with Tom and Nan for the wedding of Beryl and Jim's eldest son, Lantie and her husband happened to be there and she met them all again. Although Ma's golden hair had turned snow white, she was as large and exuberant as ever. She held out her arms and Lantie ran to hug her as if the years between had never existed.

CHAPTER 11

Priors Ings

Lantie applied for a teaching post at the Church School in Priors Ings. It was the same school which her grandfather had built in the nineteenth century and the one she attended as a child.

She came home from Liverpool at half-term for an interview. This was scheduled to be held at the Vicarage on the Friday evening. Before the meeting she accompanied the Canon on a visit to two members of the Board of School Managers who would be unable to be present. As they set off, the reverend gentleman explained the situation to her.

"We are a fine company of managers, our ages make a grand total of three hundred and ninety-six years. Not many Boards of Managers can beat that, I'll warrant."

"We'll visit Mr. Sands first. He will not be able to be with us

125

this evening because of his weak chest. The night air is very bad for him. He used to be the headmaster at the school many years ago. A grand old man, eighty-five years old but still interested in everything that happens in Priors Ings."

Mr. Sands greeted them cordially and signified his approval of Lantie by saying, "Of course she will be suitable for the post. I used to teach her mother, years ago. She was a bright lass, went on to grammar school, as I remember."

Later they went to see Mr. Franks who was eighty-nine and even more frail than his fellow manager. He was amazed that they should need to consult him at all. "I've known the family all my life. Knew her grandfather. Yes! She must have the job."

When they left Mr. Franks' house, the Canon said, "I don't suppose old Mr. Hogg will be at the meeting. He is ninety-eight. He has one of these new fangled hearing aids but he cannot make it work. He lives alone, except for an elderly housekeeper, in one of those big houses on the Cowlswick Road. He is still a magistrate, Chairman of the Bench, in fact.

"Last month a chap was brought before him for being drunk and disorderly. Mr. Hogg, who stutters on occasion, was about to pass sentence. 'You will be fined t-t-t-ten s-s-sshill —' he was about to say, when the man interrupted cheekily, 'If you're not quick it will be a pound', Whereupon, without any stuttering, Mr. Hogg replied 'Tis a pound'.

"However, he will hardly come out on a damp autumn evening so that will leave the young 'uns, Mr. Thomas and myself. It should be a quiet meeting."

Lantie arrived at the Vicarage before seven o'clock. It was a cold night and she was glad to sit beside the blazing fire. Mr. Thomas, a local businessman, came in next. Then, to the surprise of the Canon, old Mr. Hogg turned up in a taxi. He was helped into an armchair, where he sat and fiddled with his hearing aid.

The Canon, determined that the business of the meeting need not be prolonged, introduced Lantie. He invited her to state her qualifications and recount her interests and hobbies. After a few questions, he asked Mr. Thomas to propose that she be appointed to the post of assistant teacher at the school.

Mr. Hogg interrupted this request. "Is she married?"

"No, but she has a young man," replied the Canon, trying to humour him.

"Where is he?" demanded Mr. Hogg.

"He's in the Forces. He's a Commando," answered the Canon. He turned to Lantie. "Did you say he was in Singapore or Hong Kong?"

"I had a nephew in Singapore. We should never have lost it to the Japanese, never, never. Now if only they had come in from the sea instead of round the back," Mr. Hogg gesticulated. "It was the guns, they were all pointing the wrong way; out to sea. Nobody expected them to come in from behind." He shook his head and lapsed into silence.

The Canon began to speak but he was interrupted.

"What's he in? The Air Force?" queried Mr. Hogg in his high, shrill voice. Then he began to mutter. "It should have been easy enough to defend but the guns were all pointing the wrong way." The Canon tried again but the odds were against him.

"When is she going to Singapore?"

Losing patience, his reverence shouted, "The young lady is not going to Singapore or anywhere else. She is coming to teach in our school. Now perhaps you would propose that she be appointed to the post."

"Eh? What? What the dickens are you talking about?" yelled Mr. Hogg, getting very agitated.

"Never mind what we are talking about. Just say 'Yes' and I'll second the motion," snapped Mr. Thomas who was tiring of the whole business.

Thus was Lantie appointed as a teacher at the Church of England school in Priors Ings.

The school accommodated sixty or seventy children, far fewer than it had housed when Aunt Harriet taught the Infant Class. There were three classrooms and two draughty porches. Heating was by means of temperamental coke stoves but in Aunt Harriet's old room, which Lantie was to occupy, there was an open fire surrounded by an old fashioned mesh fireguard.

The playgrounds were separated by a wall and rows of brick-built privies stood at the bottom of each yard. The only change from years ago was that they had been converted to water closets. One of these, in the boys' yard, was for the exclusive use of the teachers and it was kept locked. The key hung on a hook in the Headmaster's room. Lantie and the other lady teacher suffered agonies at playtimes until they were obliged to overcome their inhibitions and go indoors and ask for it.

Mr. Dingle, the Head, was a small, wiry, middle-aged man with a dyspeptic temperament. He was a martyr to stomach pains of a nervous origin. Although he was an excellent teacher, his life was overshadowed by the fear of a visit from His Majesty's Inspectors for Schools.

"They'll be upon us before we know they're on the premises," he would warn. He applied this philosophy to every aspect of school life. Poor Mr. Dingle was a born worrier.

Hardly had the children been sent out at playtime than he would bound in to Lantie's room where the morning coffee was made.

"You'd better get outside into the playground whichever one of you is on duty. We shall be in trouble if THEY come and nobody is there."

The other member of staff, Mrs. Mitton, was a very experienced teacher and she had a calm, relaxed temperament. She was a native of Priors Ings and she and Lantie became good friends in spite of the difference in their ages.

Whenever Mr. Dingle worked himself into a state, Mrs. Mitton drove him to apoplexy by saying soothingly, "It'll be all right."

His phobia about the dreaded Inspectors who, in those days, were 'Inspectors' rather than the modern 'Advisers', was fuelled whenever he heard of a visit to another school, be it miles away.

"I keep telling you two, they'll be upon us one of these days. We must be ready for them at all times."

128

Lantie used to visualise them as invading hordes of Red Indians bearing down upon the school with tomahawks raised aloft.

The ages of the children ranged from ten to fourteen years, the latter being the school leaving age. They were, for the most part, pleasant and biddable. Broad, hefty lads came from the surrounding villages to be 'eddicated', but their main ambition was to leave school as soon as possible and go to work. Many took time off for pea-pulling, potato picking and pig killings.

The whole school used to gather each morning for Assembly in the largest of the classrooms. Hymns were sung, with Mrs. Mitton playing the piano whilst Mr. Dingle or Lantie took Morning Service. Afterwards he would hold an inquisition about absenteeism or other matters.

"Where were you last week, lad? I haven't had an absence note from you."

"Please sir, it was pig killing. And pork physicked us all, sir."

Lantie tried hard to keep a straight face in the Assemblies but sometimes she had to resort to a bout of coughing or bend down to tie a shoelace to cover her mirth.

One morning Mr. Dingle, perhaps more dyspeptic than usual, upbraided two or three boys for various misdemeanours. "And if I catch you doing it again, I'll knock your heads right off your shoulders."

This was one of his favourite threats and she always avoided Mrs. Mitton's eye, as the vision of heads rolling round the classroom floor, threatened to send her into hysterics.

The humour was quite unconscious on the part of the Head. A monitor who had given out hymn books was peering into the book cupboard while Mr. Dingle waited to start the service.

"What are you doing, lad?" he bellowed.

"Please sir, I'm looking for The Land of Many Delights."

"Then find it and get back into your line."

Mrs. Mitton and Lantie often feared he would one day burst a blood vessel although they too did their share of shouting and chastising.

On one occasion Lantie, irate at some piece of impudence, brought two boys to the front of the class. There she proceeded to whack their outstretched hands with a ruler. In the midst of this performance the rear door of the classroom opened and two strange men started to enter.

"Oh, sorry. You're busy, I see," grinned the first one. "We'll come back later." Behind them Lantie glimpsed the pale, horrified face of Mr. Dingle. His worst fears had been realised and His Majesty's Inspectors were on the school premises.

While the two men were in Mrs. Mitton's room, he dashed in to see Lantie.

"We could hear those whacks all over the school," he said. "I warned you time and again. Don't say I didn't warn you."

"They were being impudent and would not get on with their work. They deserved to be walloped. I shall tell the Inspectors so if they say anything," retorted Lantie.

When the men came into her room no mention was made of earlier events. They looked at the notebooks, questioned the children, studied the pictures and apparatus around the room and listened to a lesson on local history.

When the men had departed and the children had gone home, Mrs. Mitton and Lantie waited to hear the result of the visit. It was obvious that Mr. Dingle was greatly mollified by the Inspectors' report.

"Yes, they were quite pleased. I think I can safely say that they were very pleased with the work we are doing here. They liked your Local History schemes and all the information the children had gathered about Priors Ings," he reported to Lantie. "Did they say anything to you about whacking those lads?"

"No! I expect they thought the boys deserved it," she replied.

When she started teaching at the school Mr. Dingle had impressed upon her that she would be responsible for PT and Games. He was, as he explained, 'Past it' in that department. There were few facilities for developing Physical Education, even if Lantie's interests had been in that sphere, which they were not.

After a few sessions of coaxing, threatening and bullying the children into the yard she began to see the sense of Mr. Dingle's lack of enthusiasm. At first some of the girls fancied wearing shorts and blouses. A boxful of these garments was unearthed and they were distributed amongst the eager ones. Some insisted on wearing them on top of their clothes.

The boys refused to remove even their jackets. After many wordy battles and several boxed ears, she got them to discard a few cardigans and jumpers. It was a long, wearing process and by the time everyone was lined up in the yard, Lantie felt 'past it' too. The PT lessons became short and infrequent which meant a more peaceful time for scholars and teacher.

Occasionally the children went to a nearby field for a Games lesson. This was an event even less frequent than the PT lessons. Games in the field depended on so many outside factors. The chief deterrent was a bull which the farmer allowed to graze there at intervals.

Sometimes a horse was wandering among the trees in the distance. This animal had a bad reputation. Rumour had it that the creature had once bitten a postman. What he was doing in the field was unclear, but the presence of the horse was enough to cancel the lesson. From time to time the farmer informed Mr. Dingle that he wanted to grow a crop of hay so the field would be out of bounds. The playgrounds were not a satisfactory substitute so the Games lessons at the school left much to be desired.

The war had been over for some sixteen months when Lantie returned to Priors Ings. Mama, Poppa and Uncle Tobias were a few years older than when she had left home but life went on as smoothly as it had done during her childhood. Than was away at college and came home at weekends.

Phoebe had married, had a baby and moved away. Emmy, faithful and willing as ever, had come back to clean for Mama when her wartime job finished.

Rationing was still tight but some restrictions were lifted. Travel became easier so, in 1947 Lantie and three of her friends together with Than, went abroad for the first time in their young lives. They went to Switzerland.

There were no package tours and they made all the arrangements themselves, writing to the Swiss Embassy for information and advice. The travel allowance was twenty-five pounds each, which had to cover everything. Somehow they managed to spend three weeks abroad on this money, the exchange rate being an amazing twenty-six Swiss francs to the pound.

Switzerland seemed like a paradise after wartime and postwar England. The young people were overwhelmed by the bright, clean towns and the shops packed with luxury goods. They had travelled through grey, war-torn France to the Swiss border. As they boarded a clean, shining train in Basle, everything changed. They journeyed towards Lucerne and saw, for the first time, the wonderful Swiss scenery. To the amusement of the other passengers, they ran from side to side of the carriage, exclaiming and calling to one another in their excitement.

From the hotel in Hergisvil, below Mount Pilatus, they swam in the lake, paddled in canoes, walked the mountain paths, sunbathed and enjoyed wonderful meals. They made friends with some of the other visitors. Among them was an Army Captain with his glamorous blonde wife and their young son, who were on leave from occupied Germany.

One little family, mother, father and two children, looked very pale and ill. They kept apart from the other guests and responded with wan smiles to the friendly overtures of the young English party. Later they discovered that the family were survivors from a concentration camp and their stay had been paid for by a charity.

The holiday was an important landmark for Lantie and Than. It was the first time they had been abroad and it gave them both a lifelong thirst for travel.

The following summer Lantie and two of the friends who had been to Switzerland, Norah and Muriel, went to Brittany. Than stayed at home, as he was busy studying for his engineering examinations and trying to earn money from holiday jobs.

The girls travelled overnight from Southampton to St. Malo. As the ship was full they slept on the top deck, using their cases as pillows and wrapped in their coats.

The destruction wrought by the fighting in France was still very much in evidence. At Concarneau the houses and the hotel where they stayed bore the marks of bullets and signs of close hand to hand fighting. The rooms were clean but the food was far from plentiful. As they moved around the province they found that their schoolgirl French was of little use amongst the Breton people. They came home feeling fortunate that they had not lived in an occupied country during the war.

Austria was the final holiday which Lantie and the little group of friends enjoyed before they went their several ways. This time as well as Norah and Muriel, her college friends, Than and another friend, Ailia, from Lincolnshire joined them.

Although Than was still a student he managed to raise the money for the holiday by doing various jobs. One of these involved painting the outside of the Prior's House. "I'll do it for half the price you were quoted," he assured Poppa.

The latter laughed and said, "Right! I'll get the paint and you can start tomorrow."

There was some extra bargaining at a later stage when Than felt he ought to have danger money for climbing the ladder to do the guttering below the roof.

Nineteen forty-nine was the first year that tourists were allowed to visit Austria. For years after the war it was still divided into zones and each one needed documentation. Lantie wrote for details, arranged for their visas and booked an hotel.

They travelled from London by train, boat, and train again. Their foreign travel allowance was still twenty-five pounds and, like the unwise virgins in the Bible, they did not make proper provisions for the very long journey. They had to sleep in their seats as there were no couchettes available and they existed on bars of chocolate and cups of coffee, being fearful of spending too much money.

After changing trains at the Austrian border and long delays while their documents and visas were checked, they reached their destination, tired and hungry. They were warmly welcomed by the hotel proprietor and his staff. It transpired that they were the first English visitors to arrive at the hotel since before the war. Later they were joined by two or three Americans on leave from nearby Germany. Some Austrians and Germans were fellow guests.

One handsome young German, Franz, was very friendly and went out of his way to be pleasant to the girls. His English was fluent and they were attracted by his perfect manners and blonde good looks. He accompanied them on one or two walks and was anxious to learn all he could about England.

One morning Franz and Than met in the town and walked back to the hotel together. Than left him in the entrance hall and dashed up to Lantie's room where she and Ailia were getting ready for lunch.

"Get the others in here, quickly," he ordered.

"Why, what's happened?" asked Lantie.

"Never mind, just call them."

When they were all in the room Than addressed them as if they were schoolgirls.

"Now we are not going to have anything more to do with that German, Franz. I've been talking to him and I've discovered that he was in the SS during the war."

"What difference does that make? The war has been over for four years," said Lantie. The others murmured agreement.

"Lantie, don't you understand me? The SS were the most vicious and cruel of all the Germans. They tortured and killed people. They sent thousands to Belsen and other concentration camps. They were chosen because they were hard and ruthless. Franz was an officer in the SS. His hands are bloodstained."

"Oh, Than, don't be so dramatic," said Norah.

"He is so kind and well mannered, I'm sure he wouldn't harm anyone," put in Ailia. They all spoke up on behalf of Franz but Than was adamant.

"You girls can do as you like, but I shall not have anything to do with him!"

"We can't stop speaking to him. After all, he is leaving in a couple of days," said Muriel.

The other three girls agreed with her but afterwards they were never quite at ease with Franz. Although he was as charming as ever it was a relief when he left the hotel to go home to Germany.

Whilst they were in Austria they travelled by bus and train to numerous places. They enjoyed the beautiful mountain scenery and the sound of the ubiquitous cow bells. They did not meet any of their fellow countrymen and their English voices caused them to be a focus of attention.

One day, with the help of the hotel proprietor, they hired a chauffeur-driven car and went to the German border. Here, by various means including climbing, travelling in primitive lifts and cable cars, they went to the top of the Zugspitz mountain which straddled the Austro-German border.

Once on the summit they entered a dreary restaurant and encountered for the first time strong anti-British feeling. None of the waitresses would serve them and pretended they did not understand either their meagre German or sign language.

Fortunately three American soldiers were there and they joined up with the young English people and insisted that all must be served with coffee and cakes. A waitress brought the order and banged a tray on the table, leaving them to serve themselves. She stood nearby with another waitress and they muttered together and gave the party foul looks.

After they had finished their coffee one of the Americans saw some bottles of champagne behind a counter and ordered one of them. As soon as it was bought and paid for, one of the German waiters called out in English, that the last cable car of the day was due to leave in two minutes time. They all rushed out of the restaurant, leaving the champagne on the table.

When they reached the terminal there was no cable car. They walked down a hazardous path in single file to the next level. After an hour or so a lift came and they went further down the mountain. A steep path led them to the foot where the chauffeur and car waited. They said goodbye to the American soldiers.

"Too bad about the champagne," commiserated Than.

"Aw, I guess it was duff wartime hooch anyway," one replied. The girls and Than got into the car and were driven back to the hotel.

At the end of three weeks they boarded a train for their long journey home. They had to show their passports and visas as the train passed from one occupied zone to another. Just before the Swiss border the train stopped and several French soldiers came along wanting to see all papers. One of the soldiers kept Lantie's passport and ordered her off the train. Than, very worried, followed her as she was taken to a building at the side of the railway track.

There was a great deal of discussion between the military and some uniformed officials and Lantie's passport was passed around. Fortunately a French woman and her husband had been in the carriage with them. She got off the train and, after voluble exchanges with the soldiers and officials, Lantie's passport and papers were returned.

At that moment the train began to move. "Run!" yelled Than.

All three of them ran across the railway lines and scrambled up the steep steps as the train pulled away. When they were back in the carriage the kindly French woman explained that the soldiers had been looking for a woman spy and Lantie had seemed to fit the bill.

Back at home the holiday was soon only a happy memory. Than went back to college and Lantie returned to school. She and Mrs. Mitton taught and laughed together and tried to allay Mr. Dingle's fears.

"If only he would relax a bit, we should all benefit," said Mrs. Mitton.

"It seems to irritate him all the more when you say, 'It'll be all right'," giggled Lantie.

"Well, it always is all right, isn't it?" she replied smilingly.

School materials were in short supply after the war and they were kept under lock and key. Mr. Dingle examined all writing books to make sure every space had been filled before he handed out new ones. All drawing paper was counted to the exact number of sheets required and every sheet had to be used on both sides.

Materials for needlework and crafts were even more scarce and had to be used economically.

Apart from the post-war shortages Lantie found that many things at the school had changed little since she attended as a child. Often at playtime she and Mrs. Mitton would go out on duty together and lean against the wall, chatting and supervising the two yards. The boys and girls were still segregated at play even though they were integrated in the classroom.

When playtime ended the teacher on duty used to send a child to tell Mr. Dingle that she was about to blow the whistle. Then he would appear in the boys' yard ready to supervise their entry into school. At the first blast the children stood still and stopped talking. On the command 'Lines', they ran to get into straight lines and walked into the building in an orderly manner.

There were other reminders of Lantie's youth in Prior Ings school. One afternoon a week Mr. Dingle took the boys to work in the school gardens some two hundred yards away. She and Mrs. Mitton divided the girls between them and took needlework and crafts. Lantie was never very skilled with a needle so Mrs. Mitton supervised the garment making while she concentrated on simple items such as aprons and embroidery. Sometimes the girls did canework or papier maché as a change from sewing.

Naughty boys were sent back from the garden with instructions that they were to be kept occupied with useful work. Like Than long ago, they were employed making dish cloths with thick cotton and wooden needles. They were even made to chant; "In – over – under – off" until they learned to knit.

Casualties were sent back bearing messages from Mr. Dingle asking for somebody to do something about the matter. He kept bees in the garden and he and the boys were often victims of their stings. A blue-bag of the old fashioned type used for whitening clothes was kept handy to dab on the afflicted parts. When post-war supplies became easier, a bottle of Dettol graced the medicine box and served the same purpose.

One afternoon a boy was carried back to school by two other boys, having stuck a garden fork between his toes. Lantie rushed to put on the kettle. Then she cut away his sock and plunged the foot into a bowl of warm water. After the clotted blood was cleared, the wound was less serious than it had seemed and two or three plasters sufficed.

Over the years, Mr. Dingle, Mrs. Mitton and Lantie learned to work together as a team. They appreciated his qualities as a teacher and accepted but never managed to change his nervous temperament. He became more tolerant of them as he realised that they were conscientious in their work and duties.

One duty which was an anathema to all of them was the supervising of school dinners. Most children, even those from the outlying villages of Cowlswick and Gowhill, no longer brought dripping sandwiches and a slice of cake for lunch. The dinners were delivered to the school in large, heat-proof containers, somewhat similar to old milk churns. These were left in one of the porches.

At eleven thirty each morning the dinner ladies arrived and set up trestle tables in one of the classrooms. The containers were heaved through from the porch and up on to the tables by monitors, boys chosen for their brawny frames. The desks were used as tables and were covered with pieces of oilcloth and set with cutlery once the children were dismissed at noon.

The teacher on duty had to oversee the washing of hands, say the Grace and settle the children into their places. A few at a time were sent to collect plates and queue up for their food.

After the meal the children went out into the playgrounds and had to be supervised until one thirty when school restarted. If the weather was inclement they stayed indoors, reading or playing with a well-worn collection of board games. In the latter case the noise became horrendous and quelling it at frequent intervals left the teacher with a sore throat.

When they were not on dinner duty, Mrs. Mitton and Lantie hurried thankfully to their homes. Mr. Dingle left just as quickly to have lunch at his comfortable lodgings when it was not his turn to take command.

One day, as lunch time was approaching, Lantie heard a crash in the porch. She opened the door of her classroom and discovered that the two monitors had dropped a churn full of baked beans. The lid had come off and the contents were flowing out on to the porch floor. One boy bent down and started to scoop the beans back into the container with his none too clean hands. Lantie admonished them and helped to heave the churn into an upright position. Then she made them clean up the mess, all the while feeling thankful that she was not on dinner duty that day.

Playtime produced a regular crop of cuts and bruises which were dealt with by whoever was in charge. There was only one major accident during Lantie's time at the school. A young boy fell and hit his head on the ground. He was thin and delicate looking and the fall made him very pale. Mr. Dingle brought him inside to Lantie's room.

She sat him down beside the fireguard and gave him a cup of tea. After a few minutes he complained of being too hot and having a headache so she moved him to a desk away from the fire, and he put his head down on his arms.

The children came in from the playground and settled to work. Lantie taught at the blackboard for some time and then they started to do some work in their notebooks. She walked round the classroom to see what they were doing and stopped to ask the boy how he was. She looked down and to her horror she saw thick, black blood oozing all over the desk.

Quietly she spoke to a girl next to the door. "Ask Mr. Dingle to come here at once, please." He came bustling in, annoyed at having his lesson interrupted. Not wanting to frighten the other children, she led him without a word to where the boy was seated. Mr. Dingle looked aghast.

"You stay here with him. I'll send the others into Mrs. Mitton's room. I must get my bicycle and go to the surgery. I pray the doctor isn't on his rounds."

As the children filed out, one turned to Lantie and said, "Is he going to die, Miss?" While Mr. Dingle was away she cleaned up the boy as best she could with wads of cotton wool. The doctor came quickly and then returned to his surgery to phone for an ambulance. There was no telephone at the school, indeed very few schools, especially country ones, had such an instrument.

The boy was suffering from severe concussion but he did not die. He was away from school for a long time but returned at last, pale but smiling, to the great relief of teachers and children.

After more than three years abroad Lantie's fiancé returned and they were married at Priors Ings church. Most of the children from the school attended the ceremony and sang lustily during the service. While she and her husband were on honeymoon, Mama, acting upon instructions, took the top layer of the wedding cake to the school to be shared amongst the children and teachers.

Later, Lantie and her husband moved away and although she made frequent visits to the Prior's House, she never went back to live in Priors Ings. Many different cities and towns and many different schools lay ahead of her but she was unaware of them when she walked out of grandfather's school for the last time.

CHAPTER 12

Letters from Mama

The Prior's House
Priors Ings

November 12th 1943

My dear Lantie

We were pleased to see you looking so well when you came home at half term. Now that you have settled down at college and made new friends you will not be so homesick. I am glad that you overcame it, as you know how much your Poppa has set his heart on you becoming a teacher. It would have been such a disappointment for him if you had given up at the very beginning.

I am enclosing a half-crown book of postage stamps which Eva Bland gave me to send to you. Poor soul, she cannot afford them

141

but I did not want to offend her by refusing her gift. She has only her ten shillings a week pension and the few coppers she makes from her baking.

I have been buying buns and tarts from her once a week. Her home is spotlessly clean and she sets out her baking in trays on her front room table. You will not remember them but she spent her life looking after her elderly parents. Her only pleasure was teaching in the Sunday School. She is getting on in years and in poor health.

Now Lantie, be sure to write and thank her for the stamps. Tell her about your life in college. It will be something of interest to her. She was always fond of you and Than.

While I am on about the matter, did you thank Aunt Margaret and Uncle Joshua for the parcel they gave you at half term? Also, I hope you realise that Uncle Tobias always gives up his sweet ration for you and I believe he gave you some extra pocket money when you were home. Even if you have thanked him you could do so again and send him a picture postcard of the college.

I know that sometimes you think I am old fashioned but it is so important to show your appreciation of people's kindness. Saying 'Thank you' does not cost anything and shows thought for others.

There is not much news this week. We had another parcel from America. There were so many luxuries, tinned butter, salmon and dried fruit which I shall keep for Christmas so that everyone can have a share. They are still packing tea in those silly cotton bags. It must be a new fad over there.

The bombers go out as usual every night. There are a lot of different soldiers and airmen in the district; Australians, Canadians, Poles and Americans as well as our own boys.

Poppa has just looked over my shoulder to see what I am writing. He says I should not have mentioned the soldiers and airmen because the posters say, 'Careless Talk Costs Lives'. He says he likes the one that goes, 'Be like Dad, keep Mum', but of course he is teasing me as usual.

Do work hard at your studies, dear. Than will be writing to you in a few days. Uncle Tobias sends his love. I think he misses you as much as any of us.

Take care of yourself.

With love from all of us, especially your loving

Mama and Poppa

The Prior's House
Priors Ings

September 30th 1945.

My dear Lantie,

We were very worried when we learned that you and Cynthia had moved your lodgings. We hope that your new accommodation is good. The landlady, Mrs. Willow, sounds a kind, motherly person and I feel that she will keep an eye on both of you. It must be a big house if she has room for you two and her family as well as the other lodgers.

I can understand that you find teaching very tiring and not a bit like college. Remember though, it is your work and that is what you are being paid to do, so it must come first. I know that the theatres and concert halls and museums in Liverpool are a big attraction but you must put your job first every time.

Uncle Tobias has retired at last. The war years drained much of his strength but he was too stubborn to give in. Now he is over seventy and it is time he relaxed. He spends a lot of the day with his papers and books. Some mornings he goes out to visit old friends in Priors Ings for a gossip.

Than is working quite hard at school but he has to be kept with his nose to the grindstone if he is to pass his examinations for college. As you know, he is very keen on sport but that is not going to get him the qualifications he will need in the engineering world.

I cannot think of any more news this time. Do take care and try not to get overtired. Watch what you are doing when you go into the city.

Our love to you,
Mama, Poppa, Than and Uncle Tobias.

The Prior's House
Priors Ings

April 1946.

My dear Lantie

We received your letter yesterday and we were very sorry to learn of your upsetting experience at Aintree. We had all been amused when you told us that the Liverpool schools would be closed last Wednesday and anyone who wished could go to see the Grand National.

Poppa and Uncle Tobias read about the race in the paper the next day and we wondered if you and Cynthia had been able to get a good position from which to see the horses. How dreadful that you should be standing by Beechers Brook when all the horses fell there.

Your Poppa was upset to know that the officials had dragged the horse with the broken leg off the course and shot it in front of you. He says that it was done, no doubt, to put the poor animal out of its misery. No matter, it was a shocking experience for two young girls. No wonder you both say that you will never go to a steeple chase again! We hope you will soon recover from the shock. Do take care.

Much love,
Mama

The Prior's House
Priors Ings

February 1950

My dear Than,

Thank you for your letter and the photograph of you in your uniform. We were all very interested to read about your life in the Forces. Uncle Tobias said, "Why does he have to keep jumping out of aeroplanes now that the war is over?" He does not realise that airborne training goes on in peace time as well as war.

Your Poppa and I are still relieved that you were able to finish at college and gain your qualifications before you had to do your National Service. When you have finished your two years in the army you will be able to go straight into a good job.

In my last letter I forgot to tell you the tale of Poppa's suit. A few weeks ago I persuaded him to be measured for a new suit. As you know old Mr. Hanks, the Priors Ings tailor, died some time since and nobody has taken his business.

We went into town to one of those multiple tailors. Goodness knows why they call themselves by that name. Poppa was measured and then we were told to come back in a week's time when the suit would be ready.

"What about a fitting?" I asked.

The snooty young man looked at me and said in a supercilious manner, "Our suits don't need fittings, Madam. They are cut to the exact measurements and fit every time."

Then he had the impertinence to ask for a five pound deposit. We never had that sort of thing with Mr. Hanks.

The next week we went back and Poppa disappeared into the changing room to put on his suit. As I waited, a young man was trying on a sports jacket. The assistant kept telling him how good it looked and that it was a perfect fit. As last I could stand it no longer. I got up and went over to him and said, "Young man, you may think I'm an interfering old woman, but I must tell you that jacket hangs on you like a sack. It is baggy at the back and the shoulders are far too wide."

He looked at me, took off the jacket and handed it back to the assistant. As he walked out of the shop he turned to me and said, "Thanks, missus." Well, I thought, it might have been you in that shop buying a pig in a poke.

There was worse to come. When Poppa appeared in his suit, he looked like a scarecrow. The sleeves were too long and the jacket would have enveloped both of us. The whole suit only fitted where it touched him. The assistant kept saying, "We can alter the sleeves. We will put couple of darts in the trousers. We can alter it in a week."

I wasn't having any of that nonsense and I asked to see the manager. I told him that the suit was not satisfactory and we did not want it. Furthermore we would have our five pounds deposit back.

I was so angry about the whole business. Afterwards Poppa laughed and said I had frightened them all. But I knew I was within my rights. It is coming to something if we are to be fobbed off with shoddy workmanship.

If looks could have killed, Poppa and I would have expired in the shop, but we emerged safely with no suit and our five pounds. I fear the experience has put your Poppa off the idea of a new suit for some time to come.

Do take care of yourself. You say you have plenty of food so I will not send you a parcel. When you come home on leave I will make a cake for you to take back.

Everyone sends their love to you. Be careful when you are stepping out of those aeroplanes. The thought of it makes me feel quite giddy.

Your every loving
Mama and Poppa

The Prior's House
Priors Ings

May 2nd 1956.

Dear Lantie and Nick,

I expect Than has been in touch with you but I thought I would let you know that Marion had a baby girl yesterday. Just imagine, Poppa and I are grandparents at last!

The baby is beautiful and she weighed eight pounds at birth. They are going to call her Sara Elizabeth. I am so pleased because the names, Sarah and Elizabeth, occur each generation in my family going back to the middle of the 18th century. It is good to have this link down through the years.

I think Than and Marion would like you both to be godparents to the baby. They are planning to have the christening here in Priors Ings church. I hope it will be a fine day so that we can have the christening party out on the lawn.

I am sorry that this is such a short letter. We are looking forward to seeing you both next weekend.

Our love to you

from Mama and Poppa.

The Prior's House,
Priors Ings

May 18th 1959

Dear Lantie and Nick,

As I told you on the 'phone, Than and Marion have another little girl. She is beautiful, very fair with downy blonde hair, quite a contrast to dark-haired little Sara. Your Poppa and I are delighted to have another granddaughter.

We hope you will be able to come up for the christening, although I know it is a long journey for you.

Poppa and I were sorry to learn that you will be moving even further away. Of course we realise that you must go when there is the opportunity of another promotion, but we miss you living close to us.

As usual Poppa looks on the bright side. He says that we shall be able to visit you and see yet another part of the country. Now that he has retired and poor Uncle Tobias has gone we can come to you more easily than you can come to Priors Ings.

I expect you will soon get another teaching post, Lantie, when you have settled in your new home. You will be fairly close to London so you will be able to go to the theatres quite often. I do not go to Leeds as much as I used to do. We watch a lot of plays and musicals on the television. Some of them are very good but others are quite ridiculous.

I forgot to thank you for last week's letter and telephone call. It must be the excitement of seeing the new baby and the news of your move that has made me absentminded.

Take care of yourselves, my dears. We look forward to seeing you quite soon,

Your ever loving

Mama and Poppa

Brantford,
Ontario
Canada

July 1964

My dears,

As you will realise, we have arrived safely in Canada. Betty and Wray met us at Toronto Airport and we had a long drive to their home. Because of the time difference we were very tired and confused by bedtime and we slept until late the next morning.

We enjoyed the flight. I know you told me not to look out of the window when the plane was taking off and banking but I did so and it was very exciting. The wings were opposite our window and there was no movement from them at all. No! I did not expect them to start flapping, but they seemed quite rigid.

We had a lot of food on the plane. It was served in containers divided into sections. Some of the dishes were a bit tasteless but it was an experience.

Now that we are rested we are looking forward to meeting the members of Poppa's Canadian family.

Thank you for all you did in arranging for us to come here. We should never have managed everything on our own. It still seems like a dream and we keep assuring each other that we are really and truly in Canada.

I hope that Penny is behaving and that she is not too much trouble when you take her for her walks. Please do not overfeed her or she will put on too much weight. One meal a day and a few small dog biscuits will be enough for her.

We hope you are both well. I will write again in a few days.

With much love

from Mama and Poppa

Brantford
Ontario
Canada

August 1964

Dear Both,

We have been having such a busy time that I am afraid I did not write to you last week. Everyone is so hospitable and there are so many places to visit and people to meet.

We visited Niagara Falls about ten days ago. What a wonderful sight it is! The Canadian Falls, which are shaped like a horseshoe, are more magnificent than those on the American side of the border, but the whole spectacle is amazing. There was a boat called *The Maid of the Mist* which went right under the Falls. Poppa wasn't sure whether it was the same boat as the one he went on all those years ago, but it had the same name.

One day we went to the Bell Homestead where Alexander Bell, the inventor of the telephone lived. It is quite near to Betty and Wray's home.

Brantford is called The Telephone City and there is a big tower displaying this message. It was all very interesting but the place that interested me most was the birthplace of Adelaide Hunter Hoodless, the founder of the Women's Institutes. I bought a lot of postcards and pamphlets to show the members of our W.I. in Priors Ings when I get home.

Last Sunday we went to a big barbecue and met all the family. Betty's brother Jim and his wife Helen have five children and some of them are married with little ones. There were so many young people there and they all made us feel so welcome. Next week we are going to stay with Jim and Helen on the farm.

The weather here is beautiful and we can set out for the day without having to worry whether we shall need our macintoshes or not.

You cannot imagine the variety of foods in the shops and the wonderful meals we have had. Sometimes people drop in unexpectedly and stay for supper. Often as well as Betty and Wray and their three children and ourselves there are as many as a dozen more sitting down to eat. Betty is very calm and efficient and she takes all this in her stride.

When we experience the warmth of the hospitality over here, I feel that my own leaves a lot to be desired. As you know, I have always loved to have visitors but my efforts seem meagre compared with the welcome we have been shown here. Such kindness brings a lump to my throat.

Take care of yourselves, my dears. I will write again next week.

Ever your loving

Mama and Poppa

Brantford
Ontario
Canada

August 1964.

Dear Lantie and Nick,

Thank you for your letter and Poppa's birthday card. We were pleased to know all is well with you and that Penny is behaving herself.

We have been staying with Jim and Helen out at the farm. It is a delightful place and they made us very welcome.

When we came back to Brantford there was an invitation for us to go to Toronto to stay with Mr. Dunne, your Poppa's old boss. Wray and Betty drove us to the city.

It brought tears to my eyes to see Mr. Dunne greet Poppa after so many years. He and his wife made us feel at home from the first minute we met them. They took us to see the sights of the city and we went out to dine in very expensive restaurants.

Their house was quite an old one as houses go in Canada. It was full of beautiful antiques. They had a cook who produced the most wonderful meals, but otherwise they seem to live very simply.

Mr. Dunne and your Poppa spent hours and hours talking about the Old Days. They were like two schoolboys together. Mrs. Dunne is reserved but very friendly. She comes from one of the old Toronto families and I had all her family history while the men were talking.

We met two of Mr. Dunne's children who are grown up with families of their own. They were just babies all those years ago when your Poppa worked for him.

We are having the most wonderful holiday, but for me the best part of it is seeing your dear Poppa so happy. Do you remember, Lantie, how he used to tell you and Than stories about Canada when you were little? He used to say that we would come one day but I thought it would always remain a dream. Now we are really here and Poppa's dream has come true. We have seen all the places he used to describe and a lot more as well. We shall remember this holiday for the rest of our lives.

Yesterday, as you know, it was Poppa's birthday and Betty and Wray gave a party for him. After the meal he was handed a large box, beautifully wrapped and decorated with a big bow of ribbon. When he removed the outer paper, a label on the box said, 'Cheese'. As you know it is the one food he cannot bear to eat or even have it near to him on the table. However he went on opening the box and inside several more lots of wrapping paper there was a camera! It was such a happy day for him.

Tomorrow we are all going out to the farm for a Pig Roast. It will be the last family party before we leave for home. I can hardly believe that we have been away all these weeks and that we shall be back in Priors Ings in a few days.

I must close now as we have visitors again.

With much love from

Mama and Poppa

Call Back Yesterday

Priory Garth
Priors Ings

June 1968

My dears,

What a worry this house hunting business is, to be sure. It is good of you all to take so much trouble to find us a place near to you. We realise that the time is coming when we shall have to move from Priors Ings. We cannot expect you to drop everything you are doing and come chasing up here whenever there is a crisis. I fear that I panicked when Poppa had to go into hospital last year. It was such a relief when the four of you came up so quickly, especially as you are all so far away.

I know that we have looked at a number of houses near to you and near to Than and Marion as well, but none of them seemed quite right for us. We do not fancy living on an estate, even if the houses are new and well equipped. The only two places we really liked were far too isolated. We have to face the fact that we need to be near to civilization now that we are getting older.

Oh, if only we could take up our bungalow out of the orchard and put it down in your garden! When we have been away we are so happy to get home again and we do not want to leave it.

I know that we shall have to make a decision soon. Please keep on looking at houses and we will come down in a few weeks time to see if there is anything suitable.

I must close now and go to the Mothers Union. Your Poppa has a meeting of the Parochial Church Council tomorrow night. We shall miss all our interests and our friends in Priors Ings when we move. We have had such a happy life here, for which we are both so thankful. Now we must prepare for the changes and upheavals ahead of us.

Thank you for all your kindness to us,

Your ever loving

Mama and Poppa.

CHAPTER 13

Changes

"We must do something, they are not getting any younger. In fact they seem more frail each time I see them. Priors Ings is a long way off when one of them is ill. They will have to come nearer to one of us."

Than looked and sounded worried. He and Lantie were having their umpteenth discussion about persuading Mama and Poppa to move.

"It's going to be hard for them to leave," said Lantie. "Mama has lived in Priors Ings all her life and Poppa has been there for over fifty years, even if he is still an Incomer. They like the idea of moving close to us but the reality would be quite different. Think of the upset and upheaval."

"It's better to have the upset now while they are still active and there are two of them. Imagine the trauma if one is left up there alone. We must find somewhere soon," replied Than.

By the late sixties, after both of them had moved several times to different parts of the country, Than and Lantie were living in the south of England, only twenty-five miles apart from each other. Each time Mama and Poppa came down to visit them, they warmed to the idea of moving house. When they went back home to Priors Ings, the plan seemed less attractive. Finding a suitable place for them was not an easy matter.

"I'm fed up looking at houses," grumbled Lantie. "When they come down here, we collect literature from various house agents and tour the district. The ones I think are suitable, they don't like at all and the ones they want simply won't do."

"I found a very pleasant bungalow in a small close. It was among half a dozen specially built for elderly people. They both rejected it out of hand. Poppa said they couldn't possibly live there, it would be like living in a beehive. Mama informed me that they didn't want to be amongst a lot of old people, they liked young company. So that was the end of that property."

"The only one they really liked was a house way out in the country. It had an enormous garden and was two miles from the nearest village. It might have been alright while Poppa is still driving his car and can cope with the garden. But how long will that be?" Than nodded in agreement.

"If we don't find something soon, they will lose all interest in moving and will stay in Priors Ings. Then, when one of them dies, the other will have to come down here and live with each of us in turn."

"Yes, it would be far better if they could move while they are both active," said Lantie. "They would have the pleasure of seeing your children grow up. They could spend much more time with all of us and have an enjoyable life in their declining years."

A few weeks after this conversation Than telephoned Lantie. "I think we have found a house near us which would suit Mama and Poppa. It's an old place which has been divided into two flats and there is a long garden at the back. It is only a mile or so from our house and a couple of minutes walk from the common. They can take their little dog out three times a day if they feel so inclined. Can you come over on Saturday and see what you think about it? A lot of work needs doing to the property but I think it is what we have been seeking."

At the weekend Lantie and her husband went over to view the house. They met Than and his wife and all four of them agreed that it would be suitable for Mama and Poppa.

Than had a friend whose widowed mother would like to rent the upstairs flat. As they wandered round the property and the garden they all felt hopeful and enthusiastic.

"We'll get them down here next weekend and see what they think about it," said Than. "Frankly if they won't have this place I feel like giving up the hunt and letting them stay in Priors Ings. We are like you, fed up to the teeth with house hunting."

Mama and Poppa came down a few days later. They did not enthuse over the house but wandered round quietly, looking at everything. They walked down the garden and back into the downstairs flat. They looked at each other and then at their children. It was Poppa who said "Yes! I think we could settle here." They all beamed at him.

Some years earlier Mama and Poppa had sold the Prior's House and moved into a bungalow which they had had built in the orchard. Here, surrounded by garden and trees, they had lived happily throughout their seventies. Now the time had come for another, more drastic move.

There was much work to be done on the flats before they were ready for occupation. Every weekend Lantie and her husband drove over to meet Than and his wife and young daughters there. One or two friends were press-ganged to help.

Than, a Do-It-Yourself enthusiast, was in charge. He was a perfectionist and insisted that the whole property be overhauled and decorated. Baths, washbasins and lavatories were ripped out and replaced. Plumbing and electric wiring was renewed. Outside drains were checked and new stone slab paths were laid. When all the big jobs were done the insides of the flats were papered and painted.

"It won't do, Lantie. You need another coat of paint on that door. Rub it down and go over it again." Lantie flung down her paint brush in exasperation.

"Than, I've put three coats on it already. For goodness sake, we're not getting the place ready for the Queen Mother to live in," she snapped.

"If you're going to do the job, do it properly or leave it alone," he retorted. Lantie muttered to herself and picked up the paintbrush to tackle the door once again.

"The trouble with him is that everything has to be perfect," she grumbled to her husband who was working nearby.

At last the two flats were ready for occupation. Mama and Poppa sold their bungalow quite quickly and moved into their new home with only a few minor disasters and breakages.

Everyone was so busy getting them settled in that there was no time to enquire how they felt about leaving Priors Ings. No one asked Mama if she had shed tears on saying goodbye to her old friends. No one wondered if she was heartbroken at leaving the place where she was born and had lived for nearly eighty years, the place where generations of her ancestors slept in the churchyard alongside Uncle Tobias.

An old lady, Mrs. Dobbs, moved into the upstairs flat and they all began a new life together. Poppa was happy tending the garden in which there were soft fruit bushes, apple trees, a vegetable plot, a lawn and flower beds. At the front of the house was a small rockery and flower garden with stone steps winding upwards through it to the front door.

Mama quickly made friends with Mrs. Dobbs and became acquainted with their neighbours. She and Poppa attended the nearby church and soon had a circle of acquaintants. People dropped in for coffee or came in the evenings for a hand of cards or a game of Scrabble.

Mama and Poppa frequently reassured one another that they had done the right thing in moving. They walked their little Yorkshire terrier on the common each day. They saw Than and his wife and their granddaughters very often. Lantie and her husband visited them once a fortnight and Mama and Poppa went to stay with them during the school holidays and at Christmas. Poppa still drove his car and they were able to explore the nearby towns and surrounding countryside.

Life was good, they told each other and the family. Only on occasions when she was feeling under par did Mama shed a few tears and wish that she could go back to Priors Ings. Then, Poppa, who was ever optimistic, would gently cheer her up again.

Her chief contact with Priors Ings was through the letters of her good friend Kathy. Every month without fail an epistle arrived full of news, gossip and comments on local and national affairs. They were long, interesting letters and they were passed round the family like religious tracts.

"It is much better than having a local paper. We get all the Priors Ings news from Kathy, not just a paragraph or two," Mama used to remark.

When Lantie came to visit them she would ask "Have you had a letter from Kathy?" Then she settled down to read it whilst Mama made coffee.

Yet Kathy and her husband, George, were not natives of Priors Ings. They had come to the little town after George left the Air Force at the end of the war. They were both friendly but forthright Yorkshire folks and they established a thriving business in the place. They settled into the community so well, that in time people forgot that they were Incomers and regarded them as Priors Ingites.

It was with these good friends that Mama and Poppa stayed when they went back to visit their old home. In turn, they and other friends made the long journey south to see new surroundings and to renew old ties.

Once they were well settled, Mama and Poppa set out to visit places they had wanted to see but never got round to visiting. Scotland, Cornwall and Wales became their holiday destinations.

Their trip to Canada was never repeated but it was a subject about which they reminisced for the rest of their lives. These memories were revived when different members of the Canadian branch of the family came over to see them.

Living close to Than and his wife and children had many advantages. They were happy to babysit with the growing girls and they joined in all the family anniversaries and gatherings. It was at Than's house they celebrated their Golden Wedding, with friends and relations coming from far and wide.

In addition, being near to Than was useful for life's little dramas and emergencies. One night they had been watching television until quite late. Poppa switched off the set and they prepared to go to bed. He called to the little dog and went to the back door to let her out into the garden for a last run round. There was no response from the dog basket. When they investigated they found their beloved pet lying dead.

Than had gone to bed when a frantic telephone call summoned him to deal with the crisis. He arrived at the house, went straight to a cupboard and took out a bottle of brandy. He poured a restorative measure for each of his distraught parents and one for himself.

Later, when they had calmed down, he took the little corpse away with him and buried it in his own garden the next day.

About a month after this distressing incident, Lantie went over on her fortnightly visit to Mama and Poppa. She was met at the gate by a yapping Yorkshire terrier. Mama hurried out, all smiles, to explain the animal's presence.

"Than found her for us. She belonged to an old lady who couldn't cope with her. She was in her eighties. So we were asked to take her. Isn't she a beauty?"

Mama blissfully ignored the fact that she and Poppa were both in their eighties. The walks on the common were resumed, to the satisfaction of the dog and her new owners.

A few years after moving from Priors Ings, Poppa had a slight heart attack. He spent a night in hospital but he was soon out and about again. Nonetheless he regarded it as a warning and decided, very reluctantly, to give up his car. He had been driving since 1910 and belonged to the Veteran Drivers Club. The blue and gold V-shaped badge, bearing the number 63 in the centre, was one of his most treasured possessions. It represented all the years of his long love affair with engines and cars.

After so long at the wheels of numerous vehicles, Poppa missed driving. Than and Marion took them wherever they wanted to go. When Lantie and her husband visited they took them for drives in the countryside. They all knew that, for Poppa, it was not the same as being behind the wheel. He bore the loss philosophically as he had done all his problems in life and, as ever, he counted his blessings.

In March 1976 Lantie went to Greece with three friends. On her return she was met at the airport by her husband and the news that Poppa had had a stroke. They dashed over to see him and found that he was making strenuous efforts to recover.

Than's wife, Marion, played a major part in nursing him back to health. In addition she looked after Mama who could never cope with other people's illnesses at the best of times. Marion's help meant that Poppa was able to stay at home instead of going into hospital. The District Nurse, who called every day, was very impressed by the care he was receiving. She told Mama that Marion would have made an excellent nurse.

Poppa's will-power was astonishing and within a month he had recovered his speech and regained the movement in his limbs. After a few more weeks, he and Mama were taking the dog for walks on the common and he started to garden again.

Whilst he was convalescent Lantie used to go over each week to help in various ways. She spent a lot of time playing draughts with him. He took a long time to make the moves but the effort helped to exercise his brain. Later he was able to play his favourite game of Scrabble. As the weeks went by he enjoyed once more pitting his wits against hers.

By early Autumn Poppa seemed back to normal. He took an interest in reading the newspapers, in family affairs, Than's business and the children's education. Only his face showed how much he had suffered. His brown eyes still twinkled but he looked drawn and thin and was obviously failing.

The Canadian cousins, on hearing of his illness, dashed over to see him as fast as they could make arrangements for a flight. Their visit cheered him immensely. Poppa, who was always so kind and thoughtful himself, appreciated kindness from others.

One October morning, about six o'clock, the telephone rang in Lantie's house and she answered it.

"Lantie, it's Than. Bad news. Poppa died in the night. It was very sudden but peaceful. We have brought Mama over to our place. Can you get over here as soon as possible? I'm at Heathrow on my way to Amsterdam but I'll be back this evening."

In the background Lantie could hear the departures and arrivals being announced. She held the phone without speaking. "Lantie, are you all right?"

"Yes, Than. I'll get over as soon as I can. I shall have to ring the school and get time off. Go now or you will miss your plane. I'll see you this evening."

At first Mama was too numb with shock for tears. She kept telling each and everyone about the happy day they had spent together.

"Your Poppa gardened all morning and in the afternoon he went down into the village to have his hair cut. Mrs Dobbs and a friend came in for supper and afterwards we played Canasta. We went to bed quite late. Poppa woke me about two o'clock and asked me to open the window. When I got back to the side of the bed, he looked up at me and said 'Goodbye, my love'. Then he was gone."

Mama spoke in terms of disbelief. The tears came later. She never went back to live in the house near the common, but spent the remainder of her days in the Granny Annexe at Than's house.

After the funeral, Lantie and Than went to the flat to collect some things for Mama. They stood for a while at the French windows and gazed down the garden.

"Look, Lantie. There's Poppa's little robin, the one that used to follow him around when he was gardening," said Than. Lantie looked at the bird and then she began to weep.

"Oh, Poppa, Poppa," she cried. Than put his arm around her shoulders and drew her to him.

"Don't cry, Lantie. Try to remember him as he was in his prime and all the happy years we had together. Think how lucky we were to have had him for so long. We were lucky – – – so very lucky – – –."

CHAPTER 14

Stockholm to Heathrow, 1989

"Wake up! Wake up! We shall be landing in a short time."

For the second time that day Than was roused from a deep sleep. On this occasion he found one of his fellow passengers digging him in the ribs.

"I didn't wake you when the meal came around. Guessed you could do without it. If there was a prize for the worst airline food, this one would win hands down. You seemed kinda troubled in your sleep. Maybe I should have woken you earlier," said the American.

"No! Everything's fine. I was dreaming, just dreaming," replied Than.

"We're dropping down on the flight path and are pretty close to Stockholm. Feel the fuselage, it has cooled down. Now I reckon that is strange, very strange."

Than put his hand to the side of the aircraft and found that it had indeed cooled down.

"Remind me never to travel on a Russian plane again," said his companion.

"There are times when I can't avoid it and this is one of them," laughed Than.

They talked in a desultory fashion with the others until the time came to fasten their seat belts prior to landing at Stockholm International Airport.

"Are you guys old enough to remember the old wartime song 'Coming in on a wing and a prayer'?" joked one of the Americans.

Shortly afterwards they landed safely and were seen off the plane by the sturdy Russian stewardess. Than bid farewell to his fellow travellers and went to check his flight to Heathrow. He found that he had more than two hours to wait, so he went to a restaurant and had a substantial meal. Later he boarded a plane for the last leg of his journey home.

The first class section of the plane was almost empty and there were no gregarious Americans with whom he could while away the time. Than sank back into his seat, stretched his legs and let his mind wander. It was a long time since he had thought about the 'Old Days', as Poppa used to call them. All his working life had been full of frenetic activity.

Now, looking back, he remembered the love and support of Mama, Poppa and Uncle Tobias. It had sustained him from his childhood through the years to the present time. They had given him the confidence to go out into the world and carve a successful career for himself.

He recalled the stories that Poppa had told him when he was a child, of his life in Canada and America. Than reckoned he would have been delighted to know that, between them, he and Lantie had covered a fair portion of the globe. From the Arctic Circle to Africa; from Russia to Hong Kong and China; in almost every country in Europe as well as westwards to the Americas, they had both indulged their passion for travel. He imagined how Uncle Tobias would have taken down his old atlas and derived vicarious pleasure from following their journeys on the maps.

"One more trip back to Moscow and that job will be finished," thought Than.

In the Autumn he was scheduled to be in Istanbul. Already he had made tentative arrangements to meet Lantie and her husband when they called there on their way home from Odessa and Yalta.

"Once that job's finished I'll retire," he decided. Then he remembered that someone had mentioned an assignment in India, a project which might be interesting. But maybe he would forego that one and settle down to a less hectic life.

He cast his mind back to the seventies and the family upheavals of that period. To Mama, who had lost all motivation for living after Poppa died. He remembered Lantie remarking to him, "I don't know why people say that children are a comfort in one's old age. After Poppa had gone, Mama's reason for living had gone too. We were not really a comfort to her. No matter what we did to help her, she wanted only one thing, to join Poppa." A benevolent deity had decreed that Mama had her wish within eighteen months.

Than pondered on the other highs and lows of his life: the marriages of his two daughters; his wife's serious illnesses and his own health problems and finally the birth of his beloved, long awaited grandchildren.

"I've been very lucky. I've had a good life," thought Than.

Certainly he had all the trappings of success; a large house; a boat designed and built to his own specifications; a vintage car and a couple of modern ones. Yet there was always the driving energy which would not let him rest. He knew that, even if he retired, he would need plenty of tasks to keep him busy. He would miss all the travelling, tiring though it was at times. Still, he could make frequent visits to Canada and America and see all his friends and relations. He could go on his annual pilgrimage to the Indianapolis Grand Prix, although that would not be enough to satisfy his itchy feet.

He would, Than decided, make an effort to keep in touch more closely with his old friends. He regretted that, in some cases, the ties between them had weakened over the years. Maybe they had been busy through the decades as he had, with their careers and families. Soon they would all be of retirement age and then they could get together and remember the past.

A few lines from a poem he had learned at school came into his head.

> "And the men that were boys
> When I was a boy
> Will sit and drink with me."

Yes! He would pick up the threads from the old days once he had retired. If he retired, he thought, wryly.

"And when my grandchildren are old enough I'll tell them stories of Priors Ings, and Mama, Poppa and Uncle Tobias. I expect they'll enjoy hearing about the days when grandad was a boy."

As the plane touched down at Heathrow Than looked at his watch. It was twenty-two hours since he had left the hotel in Moscow. He collected his luggage from the carousel and went to find a telephone in order to ring his wife.

Then he picked up his cases, hurried through Customs and across the concourse. He hailed a taxi and, as he settled in the back of it, all the tiredness seemed to drop from him. He relaxed and smiled to himself, happy in the knowledge that he would soon be at home with his loved ones.

THE END